Deacons
and the Church

Deacons
and the Church

Owen F. Cummings

Paulist Press
New York/Mahwah, N.J.

Acknowledgment
The author thanks the Paulist Press and, in particular, Kevin di Camillo for his editorial guidance.

Scripture extracts are taken from the New Revised Standard Version, Copyright © 1989, by the Division of Christian Education of the National Council of the Churches of Christ in the United States of America and reprinted by permission of the publisher.

Quotations from Walter Abbot's edition of *The Documents of Vatican II* © 1966, are reprinted with permission of America Press.

Cover design by Sharyn Banks
Book design by Lynn Else

Library of Congress Cataloging-in-Publication Data

Cummings, Owen F.
   Deacons and the church / Owen F. Cummings.
      p. cm.
   Includes bibliographical references.
   ISBN 0-8091-4242-2 (alk. paper)
   1. Deacons—Catholic Church. I. Title

   BX1912.C86 2004
   262'.142—dc22

                                                          2004001130

Published by Paulist Press
997 Macarthur Boulevard
Mahwah, New Jersey 07430

www.paulistpress.com

Printed and bound in the
United States of America

Contents

Dedicated to My Brother Deacons

of the

Diocese of Salt Lake City

with Respect and Gratitude

for

Koinonia

Introduction

Reference will be made throughout the book to two key documents, both published in 1998, that govern and direct the permanent diaconate in the Catholic Church: the Congregation for Catholic Education's *Basic Norms for the Formation of Permanent Deacons* (abbreviated in the book as *Ratio*), and the Congregation for the Clergy's *Directory for the Ministry and Life of Permanent Deacons* (abbreviated as *Directory*).

The *Ratio* very clearly and emphatically makes the point that effective formation for permanent deacons will be closely linked to the theology of the diaconate: "The effectiveness of the formation of permanent deacons depends to a great extent on the theological understanding of the diaconate that underlies it. The almost total disappearance of the permanent diaconate from the Church of the West for more than a millennium has certainly made it more difficult to understand the profound reality of this ministry."[1]

There is no persuasive theology of the diaconate in English for Roman Catholics written by a deacon. This book attempts to contribute to that theology by attending to issues of history, theology, and pastoral practice.

1

The Mature Catholic in Today's Church

The holders of office, who are invested with a sacred power, are, in fact, dedicated to promoting the interests of their brethren, so that all who belong to the People of God, and are consequently endowed with true Christian dignity, may through their free and well-ordered efforts towards a common goal, attain to salvation.[1]

The introductory quotation from *Basic Norms for the Formation of Permanent Deacons* immediately alerts us to the overall function of the diaconate. Deacons are dedicated to promoting the interests of their sisters and brothers in the faith so that all may attain to salvation. We might paraphrase that to say that deacons are dedicated to promoting mature Catholicism so that all may advance towards salvation. What is mature Catholicism? What does it mean to be a mature Catholic? All deacons would aspire towards maturity in their own Catholicism, but what does that look like? Conservative or liberal? Progressive or radical? Old church or new church? One frequently hears and reads about these polarizations. And so, the deacon or diaconal candidate finds himself in a church marked by somewhat contrasting styles of being a Catholic. Which of these, if any, best represents mature Catholicism? As well as that, he has inherited from his parents and communities a particular style of being a Catholic, and he himself has made choices in his own nurture as a Christian that have further shaped this style. The same is true of someone who is not a cradle Catholic, but has come into the church later in life and now serves or seeks to serve as a deacon. What are we to make of this pluralist Catholicism?

The Six Styles of American Catholicism

One might claim that there are six basic styles in American Catholicism. The first four are well described by Avery Dulles, S.J., as traditionalist, neo-conservative, liberal, and radical.[2] The fifth and sixth styles are what we might call evangelical-Catholic and the new faithful.[3]

First, the traditionalist. This is not the position of someone like the late Archbishop Marcel Lefebvre, whose followers are now in a state of schism from the church. The traditionalist is someone who is definitely within the church, but sees the prevailing culture as largely inimical to good Catholic faith. Examples of cultural forces hostile to Catholicism might be movies, pop art, rock music, TV, and other popular forms of entertainment. These media and forms of expression are not inherently evil, but they are seen by the traditionalist to spawn an overindulgence in sex, violence, drugs, and egoism. To counter such hostile forces, the traditionalist wants to preserve as intact as possible various Catholic zones, such as the family and neighborhood, the local parish, and church-related schools. These are all understood as the favorable conduits of Catholicism that will transmit the identity and vision of the church to the next generation.

When traditionalism functions successfully, it produces well-informed and committed Catholics, confident and articulate about their faith. This is a good thing. However, Dulles raises some questions about traditionalism and its adequacy. He writes:

> Is it too intent upon clinging to a past that is inevitably receding? Does it equip Catholics to cooperate responsibly with other citizens of good will in building a better society? Does traditionalism tend to form schizophrenic Catholics who are devout in their personal and family life, but unabashedly secular in their professional and business dealings? Is it possible to shield young Catholics from the prevailing ethos, or does the effort to keep them in a Catholic subculture provoke them to rebel against Catholicism as rigid and obsolete? Can traditionalist Catholics accept the directives of Vatican II, which

attempted to renew the Catholic Church and bring it
more fully into the modern world?[4]

In brief, is this style of Catholicism just too counter-cultural, as
though the Spirit of God were not at work in the world?

Second, the neo-conservative. The neo-conservative rejects
traditionalism and takes a much more favorable view of what is
called "the American experiment in ordered liberty." The principles of the Declaration of Independence and the American
Constitution are judged to be in basic harmony with the Catholic
tradition of reason and natural law. The neo-conservative wants
the church to construct a religiously informed public philosophy
that will re-invigorate American democracy. Catholics have a
unique opportunity to influence American culture in this "Catholic
moment," a term associated with Fr. Richard John Neuhaus.
Catholics should avoid behaving like a marginalized embattled
minority and make a genuine Catholic contribution to American
public life. It is believed possible to do this while remaining loyal
to Catholic social teaching.

New hope and energies have been aroused by the neo-conservative movement. It gives Catholics the satisfaction of reconciling
their faith with full participation in public life. However, Dulles
asks some probing questions about this style of Catholicism also.
Are the neo-conservatives themselves too much affected by the prevailing secular climate, with its lack of emphasis on sin and the
cross? Do they set too high a value on personal autonomy and free-
market capitalism? Do they take too little account of the need for
community, sacraments, grace, and faith?

The third style is that of the liberal. Liberals also show much
appreciation for the values of American democracy, but differ from
the neo-conservative in that they would like these values to be present within the Catholic Church itself, within the inner life of the
American Catholic Church. Catholic liberals look upon the church
as a free, voluntary society, and they deplore what they see as the
residue of medieval authoritarianism. Some liberal aspirations are
the abolition of celibacy, the accountability of bishops and priests
to the people they serve, and the decentralization of authority and
power in the church. The list could go on. The liberals claim that

their agenda is consistent with the thrust of Vatican II—updating and speaking out in a friendly fashion to the world at large.

The major problem with this perspective, as Dulles sees it, is that it risks blurring the distinctive features of Catholicism. If all elements of Catholicism are reduced to their compatibility with the regnant positions in contemporary culture, what remains? A logical outcome of the liberal tendency could be the disappearance of Catholicism as it has been traditionally understood. Furthermore, the promotion of dissent weakens the solidarity of the church as a community of faith and witness. This is not to suggest that dissent has no place in the church, but rather that the facile encouragement to dissent, to do one's own thing, to think one's own thoughts, expresses a non-Trinitarian view of the person as an autonomous, thinking thing. It is to regress as a church to a Cartesian way of thinking about the person, and anthropologically to relegate the place of communion to the margin.

The fourth style is radicalism. This position is highly specific for Dulles and is not to be confused with the popular understanding of the term—that is, drastic, sweeping, rebellious, or anarchist. By radical, Dulles means a position marked by a total commitment to the Gospel, a position characterized by voluntary poverty, non-violence, and a readiness to sacrifice oneself in the service of others. This position is described as radical because it is seen to go to the very roots of Christianity in the message of Jesus, and *radix* is the Latin for "root." Exemplars of this evangelical radicalism would be Dorothy Day, Peter Maurin, and Daniel Berrigan, S.J. The radical style of spirituality inspires dedication and sacrifice for the poor and the marginalized of our society at very considerable cost to oneself.

Radicalism has the simultaneous effects of making us grateful that there are those ready to commit to this sense of gospel service, and of rendering us somewhat uneasy with such stark commitment. Using Dulles's examples of Day, Maurin, and Berrigan might give the false impression that this Catholic style is just a remainder of past grandeur. Not so. It finds contemporary expression, for example, in the views of Michael Baxter, C.S.C., of the University of Notre Dame. Fr. Baxter's brand of "Catholic radicalism" is indeed influenced by Day, Maurin, and Berrigan but echoes in today's students.[5]

Laudable in many respects, this style too has its difficulties. Because such Catholics regard their witness as almost prophetically inspired, they are often reluctant to critique their own programs or to pose the questions: "Are these the best methods to achieve what is desired? Could there be a better way of serving in terms of sheer effectiveness?" It is a disinclination to evaluate whatever the ministry of service happens to be, sometimes accompanied by a less than subtle interpretation of the Scriptures. In no way is this to downplay the contribution of such saintly radicals. It is only to suggest that human beings are radically deficient—the meaning of the doctrine of original sin—and, as a result, rigorous evaluation of our performance, moral or spiritual, seldom sits easy with us. Dulles also thinks that the radical prophetic style could lead in the direction of moral elitism. Any kind of elitism is foreign to Catholicism, as even a fleeting acquaintance with the history of the church would show. Catholicism has always been open to the mass of people and not restricted to an inner circle of the morally, intellectually, or spiritually perfect.

The fifth style is the evangelical-Catholic. This style is frequently seen in people who have been received into the church from evangelical Protestant denominations, or in Catholics who have been influenced by forms of evangelicalism. This way of being church, this fashion of spirituality, is characterized in the following ways. There is a great love of the Scriptures, which are often used on a daily basis and integrated with the pattern of life to guide and console, and to assist in the praise of God. Such evangelical-Catholics also often have a very clear sense of what they take to be the doctrinal and moral traditions of the church. For them doctrines are usually eminently clear and are there to be understood and adhered to.

These are the great benefits of this ecclesial-spiritual style. At the same time, these very benefits often have a downside to them. There is a tendency to interpret the Scriptures in a fundamentalist way that is not consonant with the official position of the church as articulated in *Dei Verbum,* the Constitution on Divine Revelation of Vatican II. Similarly, there is often an approach to doctrine that does not recognize or admit of a certain legitimate pluralism in doctrinal expression. A close acquaintance with the rich tradition of

Catholicism points up one faith, but with a variety of different conceptual expressions of that faith.

The sixth face of American Catholicism is the new faithful. In the twenty-five years following Vatican II, however it is to be explained, there occurred a vast gap or deficit in the knowledge of Catholicism and of its traditions. During this time the contents of the faith have been poorly appropriated by too many Catholics. Seemingly in response emerged the new faithful, a group made up almost entirely of younger Catholics who, for various reasons, have rediscovered their faith in a particularly enthusiastic, exciting, but traditional mode. The phenomenon is difficult to analyze. In part, it may be a reaction against the rampant relativism of their parents in faith and morals. It may reflect a vibrant rediscovery of a religious tradition in which they were poorly formed during the last two decades. Or it simply may be God at work. However one tries to gloss the new faithful, they are there, with no signs of going away. They are refreshing in that they provide new hope for the church, new vocations, and a new sense of service to the poor and the marginal. And they are challenging in that their issues are not the issues of the older liberals. In fact, their retrieval of doctrinal and moral tradition does not sit well with those who dissent from aspects of the tradition.

While the yearnings of the new faithful portend well, especially for the Catholic Church, Colleen Carroll has put her finger on the major difficulty such younger figures pose: "Young adults have a natural tendency to see life in black and white, with no room for compromise even on minor matters. And conservative Catholics often are overly alert to the missteps of those they regard as inadequately orthodox."[6] How the new faithful will affect the *koinonia* of the church remains to be seen.

These are the six faces of American Catholicism. The issue is not to condemn any of them out of hand, but sympathetically to attempt a real understanding and a real critique of what it is to be a mature Catholic. Any mature Catholicism involves three elements essential to faith and spirituality: the institutional, the intellectual, and the mystical. The terms are those of a lay Catholic theologian at the beginning of the twentieth century, Baron Friedrich von

Hügel (1852–1925). The work of von Hügel is particularly important for offering us a way through these six apparently conflicting faces of American Catholicism.

Von Hügel's Dimensions of Catholicism

It might be helpful to indicate that Friedrich von Hügel, according to his own testimony, was not always concerned with the path to spiritual maturity. What he calls his first conversion took place as a result of an incident in the cathedral at Mainz, where von Hugel watched a distraught young mother, whose baby had just died, rush into the cathedral and throw herself in despair in front of the high altar. Standing behind a pillar, he watched her face grow calm and, as she went away comforted, almost radiant. "He had watched an encounter with God, and felt that his doubts on the efficacy of prayer were ended. Unknown to herself, this girl turned von Hügel towards spiritual communion with God, his life-long vocation of prayer and the study of mystical contemplation."[7] It was von Hügel's constant engagement with the phenomenon of mystical contemplation, as well as of theology generally, that generated what he saw as the three necessary elements of religion and of spiritual maturity as a Catholic: the institutional, the intellectual, and the mystical.

The basis for the three elements lies in his view of the church as an organism. He was totally opposed to what he called "the atomic conception of the doctrinaire Enlightenment:[8] no isolationism, no cutting off of the individual from the body corporate of the church. Von Hügel wrote:

> According to the characteristically Christian conception, we start from human society as an organism—a body composing and composed of, its members, each various although constituting only one body; each powerful because powerful to give because also powerful to get, because actually first receiving much and very much; each necessary with a certain uniqueness, but this within an organism larger than itself. Already here at the start, each individual member is necessary, is various, is unique; their

liberty is not *in vacuo* or without aim or end; and their equality is not atomistic or interchangeable. All have duties, all have rights, all have service within and for the one body.[9]

Each of von Hügel's three elements of religion/spirituality is rooted in this organic conception of the person in the church. Let us consider each of the elements in turn.

First, the institutional element of religion. Von Hugel says of John Henry Cardinal Newman: "It was Newman who first taught me to glory in my appurtenance to the Catholic and Roman Church."[10] By "appurtenance" von Hügel means the dependence of the spiritual life, however intense or mystical, on the institution of the church. "Behind every saint stands another saint. In vain, do all mystics as such vividly feel their experience to be utterly without human antecedent connection. Behind St. Paul stands the Jewish synagogue and the earthly Jesus....Here is the abiding right and need of the Church, as the fellowship and training school of believers."[11] However holy or mystical a person might be, there is an *absolute* necessity for the institutional dimension of religion, for the institutional church. Through the mediation of the church, the individual is traditioned with beliefs, values, ritual, prayer—all those things that come to us from outside ourselves. The institutional element of Catholicism prevents us from becoming too emotional, or freezing into an other-worldliness. Von Hügel writes: "Complete humility imperatively demands my continuous recognition of my own multiform need of my fellow-creatures, especially of those wiser and better than myself, and of my lifelong need of training, discipline, incorporation....[F]ull humility requires filial obedience and docility towards men and institutions."[12]

Second, the intellectual dimension of religion. The intellectual dimension has to do with reasoning, understanding, making sense of reality. It proceeds by asking questions and by seeking answers that satisfy the questing intellect. It is nicely caught in some words of Nicholas Lash, a devotee of von Hügel:

To be human is to be participant in a kind of education. The history of humankind is a history of interpretative

practice, a history of attempting to make sense of our sur-
roundings and ourselves, to make the world a home.
Sometimes we learn from our mistakes. Sometimes we do
not. Often we forget the things that we have learnt. In all
this vast, diverse, often conflictual interpretative labour,
however, there are no shortcuts or final solutions.[13]

This is a very apt description of the intellectual dimension of
Catholicism. Questioning and probing are never ends in themselves,
are never ending. There is no entire appropriation of truth short of
the Parousia. Until then we are on a pilgrimage of seeking understanding and intellectual satisfaction. In this intellectual dimension
of Catholicism, teaching is a central activity. Teaching must be a
courteous activity, that is, prepared to listen and to learn in the first
instance. Teaching is not enhanced when too sharp judgments are
made, or when positions or people are prematurely condemned.
True teaching is accompanied by a profound sense of humility, the
acknowledgment that we do not know it all.

Third, the mystical dimension of religion. The mystical dimension has to do with prayer, worship, the contemplation and awareness of God. We have a tendency to think of the mystical as
extraordinary, as having to do with an extraordinary manifestation
of the supernatural. People like St. Teresa of Avila or St. John of the
Cross come to mind, masters and doctors of the Spirit. This is not
von Hügel's perspective. Rather, he writes: The mystical exists "in
some form and degree in every mind."[14] Everyone, in virtue of being
human, has a native openness to God—itself God's gracious gift—
and, therefore, a relationship with God. There is no exception.
Mysticism, the mystical dimension of religion, has to do with the
cultivation of that openness and relationship. Being mystical is
growing in continued and deepening awareness of God, and being
transformed by that awareness. One is constantly in God's presence, but one needs to be aware of this and to let that awareness so
permeate life that life is transformed.

Von Hügel offers us a most beautiful description of the mystical element of Catholicism in these words: "An absolute Abidingness,
pure Simultaneity, Eternity in God...stand out in man's deepest consciousness, with ever painful contrast, against all mere Succession, all

sheer flux and change."[15] This is the awareness of being "oned with Bliss" that Julian of Norwich speaks of. At the same time, it needs to be pointed out that von Hügel's own experience of the mystical was always tempered by the ordinariness of Catholic piety. Meriol Trevor comments: "[Von Hügel's] style of piety at once reflected and sustained his unshakeable attachment to the Church—his daily visit to the Blessed Sacrament, his recitation of the rosary, etc."[16]

All three elements in Catholicism—the institutional, the intellectual, and the mystical—must be kept fully and permanently in play. Otherwise, one's Catholicism and spirituality become at best lopsided and at worst polarized. Each element of Catholicism has its own specific temptation and needs correction through the checks and balances of the others. The temptation of the institutional element is coercive power, making others bend towards one's will. Coercive power may be immediately effective, but it never works in the long run. It causes resentment and alienation. The temptation of the intellectual element is rationalism. Rationalism is the position that thinking *for* yourself is the same as thinking *by* yourself. It is the product of an atomistic view, that the solitary self alone is the ultimate and final criterion of what is real and true. The temptation of the mystical element is superstition or what Msgr. Ronald Knox famously called "enthusiasm."[17] Unfettered emotions, or what might be called spiritual freewheeling, are a constant temptation of the mystical dimension of Catholicism.

Each element on its own, while necessary and truthful, is insufficient because it is not the whole truth. David Tracy puts it well when he says: "[E]ach temptation has been yielded to in the history of the Church; each temptation always needs to be spotted in particular situations, and healed, if possible. The temptation, moreover, of each part is to think itself the whole Church."[18] Each element is necessary, then, to hold the others in check.

Why did von Hügel think that these three dimensions of Catholicism were so necessary for the mature Catholic? His answer is that the elements seem to fit our sense of ourselves as we grow up and mature. Each element seems to correspond to the growth of the person. Take the institutional first. The child's first contacts with Catholicism correspond to the institutional; these contacts are on the external plane and are relatively passive and unquestioning. Things do not remain this way. Changes take place normally during adolescence when the intellectual element comes to the fore. Questioning, reasoning, and argument now become all important. As Gabriel Daly puts it, "Religion at this stage becomes thought, system, philosophy."[19] Again, as the person grows and matures with age and experience, room is made for the mystical element. Von Hügel writes: "Man's emotional and volitional, his ethical and spiritual powers, are now in ever fuller motion, and they are met and fed by the third side of religion, the Experimental and Mystical. Here religion is rather felt than seen or reasoned about, is loved and lived rather than analyzed, is action and power, rather than either external fact or intellectual verification."[20]

The three stages of maturity are not so much successive as cumulative. They are necessary, one for another, and one is not left behind as the person moves to the next. The relationship of the three elements in the spiritually maturing person is "one of fruitful tension."[21] Von Hügel believed in "the spiritual benefits of friction."[22] Spiritual maturity as a Catholic does not consist in eliminating the friction or tension of trying to hold together all three elements. It consists, rather, in learning to live with friction and tension, keeping the three elements in balance. This is the work of a lifetime.

Conclusion

Returning to the six faces of Catholicism with which we began, we may now read them in the light of von Hügel. It needs to be said immediately that no one face of Catholicism exists in a completely pure state. In reality there is no pure traditionalist or neo-conservative, liberal or radical, evangelical-Catholic or new faithful. They shade into one another because human beings are never entirely consistent in the totality of their lives. Nor is reality, even ecclesial reality, as cut and dried as the schema suggests. Theologian John Macquarrie writes: "The wisest theologians avoid getting themselves labeled too precisely."[23] Labels never quite match the complexity of the human person. But, having acknowledged this, one can reach a certain understanding using von Hügel's terms.

The traditionalist and the neo-conservative err on the side of the institutional dimension of Catholicism, valorizing all that the church stands for. These two styles have an insufficient degree of openness to the intellectual dimension, to the never-ending process of assimilating the tradition in successive generations through the process of asking questions. The liberal and the radical are not open enough to the institutional dimension. These styles minimize the worth of the ordinary structures of belief, value, and authority on which we all originally depend for our very absorption of the faith. They are too reliant upon their own particular vision, which, like all visions of Catholicism, is inevitably fragmentary. The evangelical-Catholic and the new faithful—despite their appealing confidence in the givenness of Catholicism's doctrines, sacraments, and morals—lack a deep awareness of the *dynamic* nature of the intellectual dimension. Yes, questions are being asked and answers are being probed, but these two styles show an insufficient awareness and appreciation of the drive to understand in relation to truth. They also show a premature dissociation from positions that are too little understood and judged to be false or even heretical.

It is into this pluriform church that a deacon is ordained to serve. Necessarily he will find himself aligned to some degree with one or more of these six faces of Catholicism and will have a natural sympathy for one or more. His ordination, however, calls him to serve the *koinonia*, the communion of the whole church, and not to contribute to the polarization that keeps too many Catholics at odds when they do not need to be. "The grace of God, which is not a quantity or a 'thing' but rather a communion with God, takes on a whole new manner for the ordained deacon, and becomes an effective burst of God's own life-force, if the deacon opens himself up to serve God and others....The deacon is working with God's own power and support through a divine communion."[24]

Diakonia makes for *koinonia*. This makes considerable demands for maturity, personal and psychological, as well as ecclesial. The following chapters will attempt to flesh out something of that mature perspective and to sketch the contours of diaconal identity and service to the *koinonia* of the church.

2

The Permanent Deacon and Vatican II

If we would really understand the permanent diaconate, we must set it back within the totality of the teaching of the Council that restored this ministry to the Catholic Church, namely Vatican II.[1]

There can be no doubt that Vatican Council II (1962–1965) was the most significant event in the history of the Roman Catholic Church in the twentieth century. Its constitutions, decrees, and declarations continue to make a huge impact on Catholic self-understanding and on how Catholics experience being church today. In some ways, unfortunately, the Council has become somewhat controversial in the contemporary church. Some speak as if there were no church before Vatican II, no ecclesial life before the reforms of the Council. That simply shows a pitifully inadequate view of church history. Others find that the conciliar reforms have gone too far and have destroyed the traditional sense of what it meant to be a Catholic. Avery Dulles, S.J., sums up the range of perspectives in these words:

> Vatican II has become, for many Catholics, a center of controversy. Some voices from the extreme right and the extreme left frankly reject the council. Reactionaries of the traditional variety censure it for having yielded to Protestant and modernist tendencies. Radicals of the far left, conversely, complain that the council, while making some progress, failed to do away with the church's absolutist claims and its antiquated class structures. The vast majority of Catholics, expressing satisfaction with the

results of the council, are still divided because they interpret it in contrary ways.[2]

The traditionalist reactionaries and the progressivist radicals of
whom Dulles speaks both demonstrate a real lack of historical perspective and seem locked into adversarial positions. However, one
of the few conciliar issues that have not been a significant source of
controversy is the restoration of the permanent diaconate, a major
achievement of Vatican II. But before we move into some of the
details pertinent to the permanent diaconate, it's important to look
at the dominant ecclesiology of the time.

Vatican II's Ecclesiology of Communion

In the ecclesiology of Vatican II and in magisterial comment in
subsequent years, the church is best understood as a communion.
Pope John Paul II in his apostolic letter *Tertio Millennio Adveniente*
shared his vision of what the church needed to do to enter our new
millennium in the full spirit of witness and commitment. He called
the church to a great ecclesial examination of conscience, and he
outlined some of the conscience issues upon which we should
reflect. There he challenged us to examine ourselves on this question: "In the universal Church and in the particular Churches, is the
ecclesiology of communion described in *Lumen Gentium* being
strengthened?"[3] In his subsequent apostolic letter *Novo Millennio
Ineunte,* he maintains even more forcefully this theme of the church
as communion:

> To make the Church the home and school of communion:
> that is the great challenge facing us in the millennium
> which is now beginning, if we wish to be faithful to God's
> plan and respond to the world's deepest yearnings....We
> need to promote a spirituality of *communio,* making it
> the guiding principle of education wherever individuals
> and Christians are formed, wherever ministers of the
> altar, consecrated persons, and pastoral workers are
> trained, wherever families and communities are being
> built up....A spirituality of communion also means an

ability to think of our brothers and sisters in faith within the profound unity of the Mystical Body, and therefore as 'those who are part of me.'"[4]

These splendid words of the Holy Father give us an important glimpse of the central place that communion ecclesiology holds not only in his heart, but in postconciliar ecclesiology. We might also advert to the brief statement of the *Ratio*: "We must consider the diaconate, like every other Christian identity, from within the Church which is understood as a mystery of Trinitarian communion...."[5] Here the vertical communion with the Triune God is given emphasis.

There are different models of what the church as communion might be and of how it is to be understood.[6] Here the most skeletal outline will have to suffice. In the fine words of *Lumen Gentium* §1, the church is "a kind of sacrament or sign of intimate union with God, and of the unity of all mankind."[7] The church is the communion of the baptized, drawn by grace into union with the Trinity and with one another to witness to and to effect the union of all in Christ. If that sounds a bit abstract, Cardinal Walter Kasper puts it very concretely and very biblically: "From Jesus Christ we have the gift of the most beautiful prayer, the Lord's Prayer. In this prayer we say and confess that we all have the same Father and we are all the children of God. A deeply moving idea. Before God and due to him I belong together with all other people to the one family of the common Father in heaven."[8] The church is a communion of the baptized before the Father, in Christ, working for the communion of all. It is this communion that the diaconate serves under the guidance and direction of the primary minister of that communion, the bishop.

The English systematic theologian Paul McPartlan puts Pope John Paul II's great ecclesial examination of conscience initiating our new millennium with Pope John XXIII's thoughts about calling the Second Vatican Council. On that occasion Blessed John XXIII said: "We do not intend to set up a tribunal to judge the past. We do not want to prove who was right and who was wrong. Responsibility was divided. All we want to say is: 'Let us come together. Let us make an end of our divisions.'"[9] The pope wanted to make an end of divisions, to inaugurate a period of renewal through this Council, to effect solidarity with the world rather than to perpetuate a kind of defensiveness, and to help restore unity among Christians. The documents of Vatican II (1962–1965) are both his legacy to the church and the charter for his vision, shared and promulgated by his successor, Pope Paul VI. The four key documents of the Council are: *Sacrosanctum Concilium* (Constitution on the liturgy), *Dei Verbum* (Dogmatic constitution on divine revelation), *Lumen Gentium* (Dogmatic constitution on the church) and *Gaudium et Spes* (Pastoral constitution on the church in the modern world). Each of these documents, albeit in different ways, shapes the meaning of the permanent diaconate restored by the Council. We shall give due attention to each of them throughout this book, but primary attention must first be given to *Lumen Gentium* and *Gaudium et Spes,* beginning with the latter.

Gaudium et Spes

The impetus for *Gaudium et Spes,* the Pastoral constitution on the church in the modern world, came from Blessed John XXIII and Cardinal Leon Joseph Suenens, Archbishop of Malines-Brussels. Suenens, supported by Cardinal Montini, soon to become Pope Paul VI, urged the Council to do more than examine the mystery of the church in itself. They were convinced that the church must attend to its relationship with the world. The Irish moral theologian Enda McDonagh rightly says that "The Constitution on the Church in the Modern World sought release from the suspicion and fear which certainly characterized the Church in Europe for so much of the previous hundred years."[10] A certain fortress-like mentality had built up in the church from the pontificate of Blessed Pius IX until that of Blessed John XXIII. *Gaudium et Spes* opened up the church to the modern world.

Paul McPartlan, a most helpful contemporary commentator on the Council, writes, "The pontificate of John Paul II has in many ways been the lived implementation of *Gaudium et Spes.*"[11] This document is marked by a positive but not uncritical outreach to the world and a concern for all peoples. McPartlan sums up John Paul II's implementation of *Gaudium et Spes:* "The Church is placed in

the midst of a world that is united by its orientation to a single fulfillment. Privileged to know of that single fulfillment, she exists to
help all to find that one fulfilling destiny. Everything she does is for
the salvation of the world of which she is thoroughly part."[12]
Putting it somewhat differently, we might say that the ecclesiology
of communion espoused by the Council is not inward-looking, is
not insular, is not defensive. Rather, the church exists as the graced
exemplar of communion with God to serve the world in bringing
that world into this conscious and aware communion.

McPartlan makes the point that John Paul II cites the following
sentence from *Gaudium et Spes* (§22) in almost every major text he
writes: "The truth is that only in the mystery of the incarnate Word
does the mystery of man take on light."[13] The Word reveals what the
human person has the possibility to become. In the same paragraph
22, we also find this: "Since Christ died for all, and since all are in fact
called to one and the same destiny, which is divine, we must hold that
the Holy Spirit offers to all the possibility of being made partners, in
a way known to God, in the paschal mystery." Every human being is
called to completion and fulfillment in Christ through entering into his
paschal mystery. "That encounter happens explicitly in the preaching
and sacraments of the Church, but it happens implicitly at some point
in the life of every human being, in a way that escapes our understanding, but is known to God."[14] We might say that the church is the
world fulfilled, the manifest expression of what creation is called to
be, and indeed *will* be at the Parousia. The church is the anticipation
in history of the end or *telos* of all creation and history, and this is
where the permanent diaconate comes in.

Lumen Gentium

Sometimes people refer to "lay deacons" but this is incorrect,
at least in Roman Catholic usage. Deacons are clergy, belonging to
the hierarchy of order in the church. As Karl Rahner, S.J., puts it:
"[The diaconate] is not a lay state, but belongs to the three official
states or degrees in the hierarchy of order itself, so that in all truth
and reality deacons belong to the officially instituted and sacred
orders which Christ founded in his Church."[15] What exactly does

this mean? How are we to understand states or degrees in the hierarchy of order?

In *Lumen Gentium* §28, the church provides us with a broad theological understanding of ministry as the ministry of Jesus Christ:

> Christ, whom the Father sanctified and sent into the world (John 10:36) has, through his apostles, made their successors, the bishops, namely, partakers of his consecration and his mission. These in their turn have legitimately handed on to different individuals in the Church various degrees of participation in this ministry. Thus the divinely established ecclesiastical ministry is exercised on different levels by those who from antiquity times have been called bishops, priests and deacons.[16]

The church understands the presbyterate and the diaconate to be different grades in sharing the ministry of the bishop. Cardinal Walter Kasper has a fine analogy that helps here: "To support him, the bishop has, so to say, two arms, which at times have different tasks."[17] Thus, the bishop has the fullest extent of the sacrament of ordination, representing the priesthood and ministry of Jesus Christ, and priests and deacons have a graduated share in this one sacramental ministry granted to the bishop. Both priests and deacons function as representatives of the bishop, all of them working to promote the communion of the church for the sake of the world. One recent student of the permanent diaconate knits the theology of ministry together in these words: "Collegiality, collaboration and communion are the backdrop for the Second Vatican Council's teaching on the ordained ministry."[18]

"*Lumen Gentium* marks out the portfolio of tasks that characterizes the deacon."[19] It is paragraph 29 that authorizes the restoration of the permanent diaconate "as a proper and permanent rank of the hierarchy" and outlines the deacon's responsibilities. Paragraph 29 reads as follows:

> At a lower level of the hierarchy are deacons, upon whom hands are imposed "not unto the priesthood, but unto a

ministry of service." For strengthened by sacramental grace, in communion with the bishop and his group of priests, they serve the People of God in the ministry of the liturgy, of the word and of charity. It is the duty of the deacon, to the extent that he has been authorized by competent authority, to administer baptism solemnly, to be custodian and dispenser of the Eucharist, to assist at and bless marriages, in the name of the Church, to bring Viaticum to the dying, to read the sacred Scripture to the faithful, to instruct and exhort the people, to preside at the worship and prayer of the faithful, to administer sacramentals, and to officiate at funeral and burial services. Dedicated to duties of charity and administration, let deacons be mindful of the admonition of Blessed Polycarp: "Be merciful, diligent, walking according to the truth of the Lord, who became the servant of all."....With the consent of the Roman Pontiff, this diaconate will be able to be conferred upon men of more mature age, even upon those living in the married state. It may also be conferred upon suitable young men. For them, however, the law of celibacy must remain intact.[20]

It is a quite remarkable paragraph, marking as it does the only article where the Council announces a future change in the practice and discipline of the Latin Church.[21] For almost one thousand years the diaconate had been simply a stepping-stone on the way to priesthood in our western church, but now a change was about to occur. The Irish systematic theologian Seamus Ryan, writing in 1968, maintained that "the basic reason for restoration as envisaged by *Lumen Gentium* is pastoral: the diaconate is intended as a means of relieving the current shortage of priests which has become critical in many missionary countries."[22] That was over three decades ago, and today what Ryan spoke of as the shortage of priests in missionary countries has become an acute situation in many developed countries, as well.

Pragmatically and pastorally, the shortage is one of the reasons for the development and widespread restoration of the permanent diaconate. However, while one appreciates the personnel crisis in many dioceses and the difficulties under which bishops labor, the shortage of priests cannot be compensated for through the diaconate. Deacons are no substitute for priests theologically and ecclesially. The 1998 documents, while expressing something of the same point of view as Ryan, admit two additional reasons why the fathers at Vatican II were keen to restore the diaconate: a desire to enrich the church with the traditional fullness of orders in the diaconate, and the strengthening by divine grace those who were already, in some degree, exercising the diaconal functions in the church.[23] "Strengthening by divine grace" is our way of recognizing God's permanent priority in reaching out to us, and, since the divine reach is sure, we are made strong, we are confirmed by it.

Deacons share in the bishop's ministry in a special way, representing sacramentally the diaconal dimension of the entire church. This diaconal dimension should never disappear, even if there were enough priests. Cardinal Suenens makes this point quite strongly: "The fact that the number of priests may be equal to fulfilling their role does not at all diminish the duty for lay people to be apostolic, since this duty derives from their baptism. In the same way, the diaconate could not be phased out even if tomorrow the crisis of priestly vocations were resolved….The diaconate should be presented for what it is: a distinct sacramental function."[24] Diaconal ministry is of the liturgy, of the word, and of charity in the church and to the world.[25]

Allied to *Lumen Gentium* is a brief but important reference in Vatican II's decree on the missionary activity of the church, *Ad Gentes Divinitus,* paragraph 16:

> For there are men who are actually carrying out the functions of the deacon's office, either by preaching the Word of God as catechists, or by presiding over scattered Christian communities in the name of the pastor and the bishop, or by practicing charity in social or relief work. It will be helpful to strengthen them by that imposition of hands which has come down from the apostles, and to bind them more closely to the altar. Thus they can carry

out their ministry more effectively because of the sacramental grace of the diaconate.[26]

Here too we see underscored this notion of God's permanent priority in gracious outreach towards us. Sacramental grace is God's action, changing and transforming those whom he touches.

Conclusion

Paul McPartlan writes: "It seems to me that one of the principal ways by which the Council made provision for living out this newly restored stance of the church *vis-à-vis* the world was by the newly restored ministry of the permanent diaconate."[27] The deacon, in McPartlan's words, expresses in several ways the "seamlessness" between the church and the world. The deacon is a "sign of seamlessness," moving with ease from the world as it is meant to be (the church) to the world in the process of becoming. The deacon is also a sacrament of seamlessness. Fortified by the grace of ordination, he is an effective agent and instrument of healing, especially for those who experience an alienating gap between church and world, between church and themselves. He is equally called to be an effective agent and instrument of healing in and between the six faces of Catholicism noted in the first chapter. Another way of expressing this diaconal seamlessness is to think of the deacon as the "and" between the church and the world, "not an 'and' in the simple way that we all are, but one with density and richness and presence."[28]

The deacon is the icon of what all in the church are invited to become. The ordained are asked by the church to embody and manifest the diaconate of Christ. The ordained deacon is authorized by the assembly of the church to manifest in his person and ministry the diaconate of Christ. Why? So that the assembly may see in their local deacon, living and serving among them, what they themselves are summoned to become.

Jesus the Deacon

*Even though more than thirty years have passed since
the Council, Vatican II, the theological understanding of
the ministry of the deacon remains unclear and con-
tested.*[1]

Often the question is asked, "What exactly is a deacon?" but
what is really meant is, "What exactly can a deacon *do?*" Three
models of the diaconate suggest some answers: the power model,
the historical model, and the kenotic model. Each model by way of
answer is important, but only the third provides the theological
foundation for the diaconate.

The power model responds in terms of the various roles and
functions a deacon exercises in the church today. The historical
model responds in terms of the history of the diaconate in the
church, especially during the first five or six centuries. It shares with
the power model an interest in describing the roles and functions of
the diaconate, but more in the past, in the early history of the
church. *Kenosis* is the Greek word for "emptying," and the kenotic
model states that the meaning of the diaconate is to be found in the
self-emptying service of Christ-in-the-church, a service that is
rooted and founded in the Lord Jesus himself.

The kenotic model takes its cue and meaning from Jesus
the deacon. Broadly speaking, the Greek words *diakonein/
diakonos/diakonia* have to do with "service." As has become clear
through painstaking linguistic research, service does not necessarily
mean menial or lowly service, especially as used in the New
Testament, but the word does signify that "the attitude of the disciples of Jesus is ever to be one of humility in serving others."[2] Self-
gift, self-donation in service of others, is the very essence of the

diaconate. Jesus of Nazareth, the deacon, is its unsurpassed and unique expression.

Jesus the Deacon

To explore what is meant by Jesus the deacon, we must conduct a lightning tour of some central Christian texts. First we must go to those remarkable letters of St. Ignatius of Antioch (died ca. 115). Ignatius was bishop of Antioch, and we know very little about him other than that he was martyred during the reign of the Emperor Trajan (98–117). As Ignatius was being taken to Rome for his execution, he wrote seven letters en route, six to various churches of Asia Minor and one to Bishop Polycarp of Smyrna. His letters provide a unique set of insights into the early church, not least into the emerging monarchical episcopate, that is, one bishop in one place. Ignatius has quite a developed understanding of what it means to be bishop, but our concern is with what he has to say about deacons.

He describes deacons as his *syndouloi*/fellow slaves in a number of places: Philadelphians 4, Smyrnaeans 4.1, Ephesians 2.1, and Magnesians 2.1. For Ignatius the deacons were his special colleagues in building up the church, and that is the force of the preposition *syn*/with. The other part of the word is *douloi,* the plural of *doulos*/slave. What does he mean by this curious term? In two passages Ignatius speaks in the highest terms of deacons. First, we read in his Letter to the Magnesians: "Let me urge on you the need for godly unanimity in everything you do. Let the bishop preside in place of God, and his clergy in place of the apostolic conclave, and let my special friends the deacons be entrusted with the service of Christ."[3] He describes a certain typology of the clergy for us here. The bishop is like God the Father, and the clergy or presbyters are like the apostles, the original apostolic band called by the Lord. The deacons are entrusted with the *diakonia*/the service of Christ. The deacons seem most closely associated with the person of our Lord. In his Letter to the Trallians we find this sentence: "Equally it is for the rest of you to hold the deacons in as great respect as Jesus Christ...."[4] This extremely strong connection of the deacons with Jesus Christ is not just the way the typology works out for Ignatius in some haphazard fashion. Rather, the connection is based on our

Lord's own self-understanding as servant, as deacon. The deacons are Ignatius's *syndouloi* because they share in a particularly service-oriented way in the ministry of their bishop. But, before we proceed to that self-understanding of the Lord and its implications, let us go next to St. Paul.

The key passage in St. Paul is from Philippians 2:6–11, a passage widely recognized as a pre-Pauline hymn to Christ. To get a sense of its hymnic nature, let us read it in poetic or hymnic form and structure[5]:

Part 1
Who, though he was in the form of God,
did not regard equality with God as something
to be exploited,
but emptied himself,
taking the form of a slave,
being born in human likeness.
And being found in human form,
he humbled himself
and became obedient to the point of death—
even death on a cross.

Part 2
Therefore God also highly exalted him
and gave him the name
that is above every name,
so that at the name of Jesus
every knee should bend,
in heaven and on earth and
under the earth,
and every tongue should
confess
that Jesus Christ is Lord,
to the glory of God the Father.

Without going into a detailed exegesis of this pericope, there are various phrases and ideas upon which we need to comment. The first is "though he was in the form of God, [he] did not regard equality with God something to be exploited" (v. 6). "Form of God" seems to mean "nature of God," truly divine. Despite the massive amount of scholarly ink that has been spilled on this phrase, it is impossible to avoid the suggestion that this is an affirmation of the divinity of Christ. This is what one might call the obvious sense of the words. Ben Witherington writes, "The term *morphe* (form) always signifies an outward form that truly and fully expresses the real being that underlies it. As applied to Christ, this means that he not merely appeared to have the form of God but that he had a form that truly manifested the very nature and being of God. This is the reason the further phrase says what it does— Christ had equality with God: he had by right and nature what God had."[6] "Something to be exploited," in Greek *harpagmos*, has the root meaning of "clutch," but "clutch" in the sense of "not taking advantage of something one rightfully already has."[7] The passage moves forward to express the incarnation, speaking of Christ "emptying himself, taking the form of a slave... [a]nd being found in human form" (v. 7). Christ is divine, but sets aside his "rightful divine prerogatives" in the movement of the incarnation. This is his self-emptying, his kenosis, the Greek verb "to empty" being *kenoō*. Paul paraphrases Christ's coming among us as "taking the form of a slave." "Slave" is the Greek noun *doulos*. While it is not the same root as *diakonos*/servant, it shares the same basic meaning. A slave or a servant spends himself on behalf of others. Christ identified himself with "the lowest sort of human—a slave, a person without any rights."[8] For Paul, no less than for Ignatius after him, Jesus is *the* deacon, the one whose life is spent for others.

Let us now turn to the Gospel of St. Mark, probably the first of the synoptic gospels, and to that great christological verse 10:45: "For the Son of Man came not to be served but to serve, and to give his life a ransom for many." The verb "to serve" is the Greek word *diakonein*, so that we might paraphrase the verse, "The Son of Man came not to be deaconed, but to deacon, and to give his life a ransom for many." The meaning is very close to our Pauline passage from the Letter to the Philippians. Christ's advent among us in the incarnation is for the purpose of service, and a service that would take him to the end, to death. When we look at the context of the verse, it has to do with the ambition of James and John, the sons of Zebedee (Mark 10:35–45). They came to Jesus and asked him for positions of power and prominence, "Grant us to sit, one at your right hand and one at your left, in your glory" (v. 37). Jesus responds by contrasting the way of rulers with his way of humble service, ending with verse 45. Jesus, setting the example for his followers, is not one who lords himself over others, nor should his disciples. "[W]hoever wishes to become great among you must be your servant, and whoever wishes to be first among you must be slave of all" (vv. 43–44). Now we can see more clearly why Ignatius views the diaconate as the characteristically Christ-like office. In Mark, Christ is the self-proclaimed deacon.

From St. Mark we pass on to St. John, and there too we shall find the dynamic of Jesus the deacon. Two passages in particular present themselves for our consideration: 12:26; 13:1–20. First, John 12:26: "Whoever serves me must follow me, and where I am, there will my servant be also. Whoever serves me, the Father will honor." As in Mark, the word "serve" is the Greek word *diakonein,* yielding the paraphrase: "Whoever deacons me must follow me, and where I am, there also will my deacon be." The importance of the verse lies in the close identification of Jesus with his followers, something that is underscored in the farewell discourses of St. John. Whoever follows Jesus is his servant, and where Jesus is, his servant will be also. They are distinct but not separate. Servant-followers are to remain in Jesus, as he remains in them (15:4). Servant-followers are told by the Lord: "I am in my Father and you in me, and I in you" (14:20). There is a close communion of Jesus with the Father, and with his servant-followers. The service is expressed in his actions at the Last Supper, taking us to our second text, the washing of the feet. At the Last Supper Jesus took a towel and washed the feet of his disciples. Foot washing was an expression of hospitality, but performed by slaves.[9] Jesus, consistent with the image of Paul and Mark, takes upon himself the role of a slave/servant/deacon and exhorts his followers to do the same. "So if I, your Lord and Teacher, have washed your feet, you also ought to wash one another's feet. For I have set you an example, that you also should do as I have done to you" (13:14–15). Cardinal Walter Kasper says of this Johannine text, "In these words one can see the foundation of the diaconate."[10]

Jesus Reveals God

In our Christian tradition affirming the Creed of Nicaea-Constantinople (325, 381), we confess that Jesus is "God from God, Light from Light, true God from true God. Begotten, not made, one in being with the Father." Jesus makes the Father known because he is one with him. The infinite, incomprehensible Mystery we call God is expressed in the person of Jesus of Nazareth. If Jesus is the deacon in his self-emptying service, as our New Testament texts have shown, and if Jesus is the very revelation of God, then somehow God must be diaconal also. The self-emptying of Jesus in service points to the self-emptying of God.

There is an oddness about this that demands our pursuance. We normally and typically think of God in terms of omnipotence and omniscience, and so we should, to express God's utter transcendence and to distinguish God from ourselves, so limited in power and knowledge. But we also need to consider the thought being developed here from the Scriptures, and ask, "How is God to be thought of as self-emptying service?" We are told in 1 John 4:8 that "God is love." It is the nature of love to share, to pour oneself out for the loved one.

Perhaps we may say that God's first act of self-emptying service was the pouring of himself out in creation. Creation came to be because God as Love could not keep existence to himself. He wanted to share existence with others, and so God, in the act of creating, poured himself out in what we might call self-emptying service. We might then go on to affirm that God's second act of self-emptying service is the Word made flesh, the incarnation. There is a fundamental congruence between the primordial outpouring of Godself that is creation and that is the man Jesus. If creation indicates the direction of the self-expressing Love that God is, Jesus is its personal performance. Jesus is God as self-emptying, self-expressing Love in person. "Whoever has seen me has seen the Father" (John 14:9).

Love is vulnerable. Love cannot demand but only invite, and so love is opened up to refusal. The history of the refusal of love is told in our own living, in the history of the world, and, *par excellence,* in the crucifixion of Jesus. William Vanstone comments:

We may say that Christ, the Incarnate Word, discloses to us, at the climax of his life, what word it was that God spoke when "He commanded and all were created." It was no light or idle word but the Word of love, in which for the sake of another, all is expended, all jeopardized and all surrendered. The Cross of Christ discloses to us the poignancy of the creation itself—the tragic possibility that, when all is given in love, all may be given in vain.[11]

The Cross was not the end of Christ, but we may not too easily pass to the Resurrection. The Cross is self-emptying Love—refused and killed.

God, Jesus, and the Deacon

The deacon as one who serves, following Jesus the Deacon, is also, therefore, one who reveals the divine nature and reality. He is called to display divinity in his life and ministry, literally to reveal the diaconal reality of God. A critical reader might respond to all of this by suggesting that self-emptying service in love should surely be the characteristic of all servant-followers of the Lord, not simply of ordained deacons.

That is, indeed, correct, and is emphasized by the *Ratio*: "[The deacon's role] is to express the needs and desires of the Christian communities and *to be a driving force for service, or diakonia, which is an essential part of the mission of the Church*."[12] However, this description does not adequately come to terms with the notion of sacramentality or embodiment. The ordained deacon represents "the diaconal dimension of the church as a whole."[13] The ordained deacon is asked by the church to embody and to manifest Jesus the deacon, so that the rest of the church may see in someone actually living among them what they themselves are called to become. The permanent deacon is both the icon of Jesus the deacon and the daily invitation to live as Jesus the deacon. All are finally called to be self-emptying servants. The deacon in his local community is the embodiment or sacrament of Jesus the deacon, and his self-emptying service is an invitation to others to empty their selves in serving. "He inspires and motivates the diaconia in the parish....His diaconal service should enthuse and thrill them, give them courage and strengthen them, so that they in their turn may serve their brothers and sisters in the imitation of Christ."[14]

The point is sometimes made that this desire to help others and to be of service to them is transcultural because it is at the heart of all human experience. This only enhances diaconal service, the deacon now being truly *catholic*, that is, a universal sign of the service to which all humankind feels called. One theologian, William T. Donovan, using the philosophy of Emmanuel Levinas, develops this insight in a particularly fine way. He writes, "Levinas has indicated in his works that the very way of life that the ordained deacon is supposed to stand for is at the heart of what it means to be Christian...to find yourself you have to lose yourself....The deacon as 'sacrament of service' is the sacrament of what it means to be truly human."[15] The deacon's characteristic and consistent self-statement is: "Here I am. What can I do to help?"

The diaconate has nothing to do with wielding power or achieving status, but is about a power-less invitation to serve the Lord. It is beautifully put by the Anglican bishop-theologian Mark Santer:

> The deacon is one who waits. He is never in charge. He is the servant of others—of God, of his bishop, of the congregation. He is a voice: it is his task to read the Lord's Gospel, not his own....He is a servant: it is his task to wait at the Lord's table....It is others who preside; he is the waiter, the attendant. Is there anything at all that is peculiar to the deacon? Is he given powers that are given to no one else? The answer is 'No.' There is nothing he can do which nobody else can do. But that is just what is distinctive about him. He has no power. He is a servant. He is entrusted with the ministry of Christ who washes his servants' feet. He embodies the service of the Lord who has made himself the servant of us all.[16]

4

A Brief History
of the Diaconate

*Today what is properly in question is not a restoration of
the diaconate in its ancient form, but a creative conception of the diaconate of the future. Ancient models of the
diaconate can provide stimuli for this new specification
of it.[1]*

Karl Rahner's words must be taken seriously. The permanent
diaconate in today's church cannot be what the diaconate was in
the early church for two reasons. First, we do not know what the
diaconate actually was in the early church; we have no precise and
detailed information that would yield us a carefully articulated job-
description of the first century *diakonos*/deacon. We should not
look at the documents of the New Testament through the lens of a
later-structured church. It took time for the ministries of the church
as we know them to emerge and to develop, although from the
beginning we can discern some kind of structure. The church was
never simply amorphous. One author comments on the development as follows: "The pattern seems to have been one of progressive institutionalization. The lines were not clearly drawn in the
early years between situations born of charisms welling up from
within the institution....The later Christian distinctions between
public ordination and private charism did not exist."[2] This summary by Norbert Brockman, S.M., provides an accurate picture of
the earliest church in respect of ordained ministry, including what
we now mean by the diaconate.

Second, Rahner is emphatic that, while what we do know or
may surmise about the diaconate in the early church may stimu-
late our thinking about the diaconate today, it should not dictate

the shape of that ministry. Our times are different, our cultures are different, and the needs of today's church are somewhat different. In a Catholic theology, this does not mean that we are free to create a diaconate *de novo,* an understanding of the theology and practice of the diaconate that plays loose with tradition. Few, if any, would subscribe to such an ecclesiological position. At the same time, however, we cannot be suffocated by the past, or we shall be unable to develop the modes of service that the contemporary church requires to fulfill her mission. The restoration of the permanent diaconate at Vatican II and subsequent developments in understanding and providing for that ministry have, as it were, heeded Rahner's words. Continuity within development is the best way to grasp how the diaconate has been restored—continuity with the past but in such a way that present-day needs are actually recognized and met. To use Rahner's word, it is helpful and stimulating to get a sense of how the diaconate developed in the history of the church, especially the nascent church, and it is to this that we now give our attention. Instead of attempting comprehensive coverage of the historic diaconate, this chapter offers a selective coverage that will nevertheless provide us with an accurate understanding.

Acts 6:1–6

Probably the most obvious place to begin our historical exploration is with this passage from St. Luke's Acts of the Apostles, regarding the selection of seven good men "to wait on tables," so the apostles did not have to do it. Since the second century this passage has been understood to refer to the diaconate. This is incorrect. "It is more accurate to see here the Church structuring its ministry but not the ordination of ministers clearly differentiated from other community leaders."[3] These words of Edward Echlin, the first Catholic theologian to provide an account in English of the history of the early diaconate after Vatican II, have been borne out by the careful, investigative research of New Testament scholars, most especially the Australian Catholic, John N. Collins.[4] Collins's work is most persuasive in many respects. He conducts an exhaustive analysis of the meaning of the word *diakonos* and its cognates throughout the classical world and then proceeds to unfold its New Testament and Christian nuances. In doing so, he has taken to task in his various writings the widespread notion that the *diakonos*/deacon was in the first century a lowly slave or servant who performed menial jobs of no great importance, someone who was involved in physical service to the needy.

The famous passage must be set within the wider context of the entire book. The entire narrative of Acts, telling the story of the spread of the good news from Jerusalem to the ends of the earth, is described by St. Peter as "this *diakonia*/ministry" (1:17). Much later, when St. Paul summons the elders of the church of Ephesus to meet him at Miletus, at the end of his missionary journeys, he tells them that he is firmly determined to finish the mission God has given him: "But I do not count my life of any value to myself, if only I may finish my course and the *diakonia*/ministry that I received from the Lord Jesus, to testify to the good news of God's grace" (20:24). And, when Paul eventually arrives in Jerusalem, he proceeds to tell the community and its leaders what "God had done among the Gentiles through his *diakonia*/ministry" (21:19). Collins comments on this use of the term *diakonia*: "Thus both at the beginning of the undertaking, that is, when the Lord commissioned the Eleven, and then at its consummation, when Paul reported to Jerusalem on his achievement, the writer Luke chooses to have us think of it as a *diakonia*/ministry."[5] The entire work of evangelization, preaching, and building up the church is known by St. Luke as *diakonia*/ministry.

From chapter 2 through chapter 5 of Acts, the Twelve are represented as constantly in ministry: "And every day in the temple and at home they did not cease to teach and proclaim Jesus as the Messiah" (5:42). Then immediately comes Acts 6:1: "Now during those days, when the disciples were increasing in number, the Hellenists complained against the Hebrews because their widows were being neglected in the daily *diakonia*/distribution of food." It is this neglect that leads to the selection and appointment of "seven men of good standing" (6:3). The Twelve were preaching the word and looking after the spiritual needs of the native speakers, the Aramaic-speaking community in Jerusalem, "in the temple and at home" (5:42). These are the "Hebrews" of our text. The "Hellenists" are the Greek speakers, who were not at home using Aramaic, and their complaint had to do with the neglect of their Greek-speaking widows, a group whose state in life made them socially and economically insecure. Collins writes: "In addition these largely illiterate Greek-speaking widows were unable to understand the Aramaic language the new teachers used. Indeed, with the Apostles so busy among the Jews, and with numbers of them not being speakers of Greek, the widows could hardly have avoided being overlooked in what Luke calls 'the daily *diakonia*/ministry.' "[6]

The Twelve respond to the complaint by saying, "It is not right that we should neglect the word of God in order to *diakonein*/wait on tables" (6:2). What does *diakonein*/serving at table mean in this context? The normal understanding has been that it has to do with food and the necessities of life, "serving at table." There are, maintains Collins, two problems with this customary understanding. First, in Luke's use of the word, *diakonia*/ministry has to do primarily with the church's preaching and teaching the good news of Jesus, as noted above. It does not have to do with waiting at table or serving food. Second, the Greek text does not actually say "waiting *at* table," but "waiting table." Collins suggests that the difference is important. The Twelve were not talking about serving food at table, but rather, ministering the word to these Greek-speaking widows, gathered at their tables. This is how he puts it: "[Luke] intends us to understand that the Twelve will not be ministering their teaching to these small groups of women on the occasion of their gatherings around their tables."[7] The Twelve ministered to the larger groups of Aramaic-speaking Jews in the temple and in their homes. But they provided ministers of the word for the Greek-speaking widows, and especially when they came together at their tables. "Therefore, friends, select from among yourselves seven men of good standing, full of the Spirit and of wisdom, whom we may appoint to this task" (6:3). And so the seven were appointed, and when we observe the work they did in the subsequent chapters of Acts, especially Stephen and Philip, we see that they are proclaiming the *diakonia*/ministry of the word.

The church finds within itself the ministerial resources to make sure that the spiritual needs of the Greek-speaking widows were met, when they were unable to be met by the mainly Aramaic-speaking Twelve. John Collins supplies us with a well-composed summary of all of this: "What we have then at the heart of Luke's history of the mission is the word *diakonia* marking the major stages of its progress. This word is there to mark the beginning of the Twelve's mission (1:17, 25), it is there at the height of their mission to Jerusalem (6:4), it is there to mark Paul's inclusion within it (20:24), and it is there when Paul completes it (21:19)."[8]

Even though it is readily conceded that the seven reputable men of Acts 6 were not historically and formally deacons, there is more to be said. One scholar succinctly comments: "Luke's readers may well have seen (even if anachronistically) the Seven as *diakonoi,* deacons in the later sense of 'holders of the office of deacon.' They may well represent the incipient stages of the later office of *diakonos....*"[9] The first to refer to them as deacons was St. Irenaeus of Lyons, writing about 185. Irenaeus describes Stephen as "the first deacon chosen by the Apostles."[10] The supportive and serving role of deacons in the local community was seen in the developing tradition as exemplified for the first time in the seven. The seven men of good standing of Acts take on a foundational diaconal role, even though they were not deacons.

Philippians 1:1

"Paul and Timothy, servants of Christ Jesus, to all the saints in Christ Jesus who are in Philippi, with the bishops and deacons." It is difficult to avoid the suggestion that St. Paul is referring here to specific officers in the church, even though from the context we cannot specify any details of those offices. It may be that, given the Gentile-Christian composition of this community at Philippi, "the antecedents of the *episkopoi* and *diakonoi* could well have been the administrative officers of the Hellenistic clubs and cult-fellowships."[11] Any social group needs some special pattern and arrangement to function at all, and it may be that the Christian community looked to an already existing, discrete corps of functionaries in their midst at Philippi. Commenting on the deacons here, Hans Küng accurately writes: "What is described here would seem to be a definite and permanent ministry in the community, associated with and evidently inferior to that of the 'bishops'."[12] More than that we are not entitled to say.

Romans 16:1–2

"I commend to you our sister Phoebe, a deacon of the Church at Cenchreae...." There is no doubt that Phoebe is described here as a *diakonos,* a deacon of Cenchreae, the harbor city for Corinth. But what precisely does that mean? Summarizing discussion on the matter, Aimé George Martimort puts his conclusion very succinctly: "More and more, scholars are emphasizing that there is an anachronism involved in giving this word a precise meaning corresponding to an ecclesiastical institution to which the first real references...date from much later...."[13] The problem is that, though Phoebe is called a deacon, and deacons occur in Philippians and the Pastoral Letters, we do not really know what a deacon *was* and what a deacon *did* at this early period. Everything that is said of the deacon and diaconate in the first century is speculation. The very root of the word obviously suggests that deacons were in real service to their local Christian assembly, but the details of that service simply elude us. On this issue we cannot hear often enough the caution of not reading into earlier periods of the church what we may know from later periods. As Kenan Osborne never tires of saying: "One must walk carefully through New Testament data, and not draw conclusions which neither the text nor the context might allow."[14]

Nonetheless, Phoebe is called both a *diakonos* and a *prostatis/*benefactor of Paul. Clearly she is very important to Paul as he draws public attention to her in the community of Rome. She is the very first named before the long list of people he wishes to greet. Reading between the lines, John Collins attempts to situate the importance of Phoebe: "Paul is in act drawing the Roman churches around Phoebe in support of the mission accorded to her by her church....This mission is nothing less than getting arrangements in hand for Paul's own projected mission to Spain, announced in the preceding paragraphs of his letter (15:24, 28)."[15] Phoebe is Paul's collaborator, patroness, and supporter, a *diakonos* of Cenchreae.

1 Timothy 3:1–13

This is the most explicit and complete reference to the diaconate in the New Testament. Notice that Paul speaks of *episkopoi*/bishops and *presbyteroi*/presbyters interchangeably, suggesting that the notion of one bishop in one place, the "residential monoepiscopate," had not quite developed.[16] Furthermore, it would also seem that the episkopoi and the presbyteroi may have performed identical ministerial tasks.[17]

1 Timothy 3:1–13 provides us with a list of the natural virtues or qualities that an *episkopos*/bishop or a *diakonos*/deacon should possess, qualities described by Raymond E. Brown, S.S., as "highly institutional," though that is understood by him in a sense that is not necessarily derogatory.[18] Many New Testament commentators point out that this list of virtues for office-holders is not specifically Christian, but is quite common in the Greek world for those who exercise local authority. However, having duly acknowledged that, the question still remains: Why is there this emphasis on character traits or moral qualities for the church's ministers in 1 Timothy? It may be that it was a serious pastoral concern, perhaps that "one of the main problems facing the author of the Pastorals was precisely the unworthy behavior of these same officers."[19] As we move through the patristic period, we will find constant comment being made on the unacceptable moral performance of the church's leaders. They were exemplars in the community, and it may be that the *point-de-depart* for this moral critique finds its origins in 1 Timothy 3:

> Now a bishop must be above reproach, married only once, temperate, sensible, respectable, hospitable, an apt teacher, not a drunkard, not violent but gentle, not quarrelsome, and not a lover of money. He must manage his own household well, keeping his children submissive and respectful in every way....

> Deacons likewise must be serious, not double-tongued, not indulging in much wine, not greedy for money; they must hold fast to the mystery of the faith with a clear conscience. And let them first be tested; then, if they prove themselves blameless, let them serve as deacons....Let deacons be married only once, and let them manage their children and their households well...."
> (vv. 2–4, 8–12)

Precisely what is meant by bishops and deacons being married only once is not clear, and commentators take up different positions. The probable meaning is that the bishop or deacon should exemplify complete fidelity and faithful attachment to his wife. Thus, Jean-Paul Audet sums up the meaning well, after discussing the various options, when he concludes that the bishop or the deacon is to be involved in a marriage that is both stable and harmonious so that he can be of good service to his community.[20] It would also seem that the bishop and/or the deacon were responsible for the finances of the community: "this is implied in the stress that he has to be able to manage a household and should not be greedy about money."[21]

"Women likewise must be serious, not slanderers, but temperate, faithful in all things" (v. 11). Then, having mentioned women explicitly, St. Paul returns to the subject of the deacons (vv. 12–13). The flow of the passage on deacons is quite clearly interrupted. So, who are these women mentioned in the passage? There are a few basic options. They may be women in general, intruded into the text here by the author. They may be the wives of deacons, and once the virtuous traits of deacons have been laid out, attention is then focused briefly on their wives. Others suggest that the reference is to women deacons, similar to the case of Phoebe in Romans 16. No less an authority than St. John Chrysostom, Patriarch of Constantinople (ca. 350–407), considers that the women are deacons: "Some have thought that is said of women generally; but it is not so, for why should (St. Paul) introduce anything about women to interfere with the subject? He is speaking of women who hold the office of deacon."[22] However, it seems unlikely that the order of deaconesses or women deacons would have been established so early in the church's tradition. Further, in Titus 2:3 we read: "Likewise, tell the older women *(presbytides)* to be reverent in behavior, not to be slanderers, or slaves to drink; they are to teach what is good." It is virtually the same exhortation to the women of 1 Timothy 3:11. It appears "the balance of evidence would seem to be in favour of regarding 3:11 as an intrusive statement regarding women in general."[23] However, it is impossible to be absolute one way or the other.

Didache

This interesting document is dated somewhere between 70 and 110, written perhaps in Antioch in Syria. We read there: "You must choose for yourselves bishops and deacons who are worthy of the Lord: men who are humble and not eager for money, but sincere and approved; for they are carrying out the ministry of the prophets and the teachers for you. Do not esteem them lightly, for they take an honorable rank among you along with the prophets and teachers."[24] The prophets and the teachers were probably itinerant charismatics, and in this passage we can see their ministry giving way to local ministers. The author of the *Didache* probably was afraid that the local, resident ministers might not receive quite the same respect as the itinerant charismatics.[25] It may well also be that the *episcopoi* and the *diakonoi* are something of a recent innovation in this community, and that "there was a not unnatural reluctance on the part of Christians to accept them as the equals of the more obviously gifted leaders, (the prophets and the teachers) they had known previously."[26] We should, of course, notice that *episkopoi* is a plural word, the implications being that we have not reached the point in this community of one bishop in one place, the monarchical episcopate.

The Shepherd of Hermas

Hermas, a second century Roman Christian, tells us in his book, *The Shepherd,* that he had been a Christian slave sold in Rome to a woman named Rhoda, who freed him. He married and became a merchant, but lost all his property in a local persecution.

The Shepherd was probably written between 140 and 155. Working through the references to the church in *The Shepherd* reveals, in Echlin's estimation, "that ordering proceeded more gradually at Rome than in the churches of the Pastorals."[27] Echlin means that the structuring of the Roman community with bishops, presbyters, and deacons seems to have taken longer than in other places. Though never without leaders, it took the Roman Christians some time to reach toward the monoepiscopate and to have clearly differentiated roles for bishop, presbyter, and deacon.

This is how Hermas describes deacons, along with other officers of the church: "The stones that are fair and white and fit their joints are the apostles and bishops and teachers and deacons who have walked according to the holiness of God and who have sincerely and reverently served the elect of God as bishops and teachers and deacons."[28] The church is described here as a building and deacons are a key part of the structure and are held in high esteem. Elsewhere, Hermas is less laudatory of deacons: "The ones that are spotted are deacons who served badly and plundered the living of widows and orphans, and made profit for themselves from the ministry they had accepted to perform. So, if they persist in the same desire, they are dead and have no hope of life. But if they turn and perform their service purely, they will be able to live."[29] The meaning is related to the list of virtuous diaconal qualities in 1 Timothy 3. The deacon has as part of his responsibilities oversight of the community's money, money set aside to look after widows and orphans who were dependent upon the church for sustenance. Hermas is aware of deacons who "are greedy for sordid gain" (1 Tim 3:9), and who help themselves to these communal funds. Whether praising or finding fault, however, Hermas's writing points to the central role of deacons in the Christian community of Rome.

Justin Martyr, Rome

Not long after Hermas we come across another Roman Christian who tells us something about deacons. About the year 150 we find this description of the deacon and his activities, given by Justin Martyr, who had a house of theology in Rome: "When the president has finished his Eucharist and the people have all signified their assent, those whom we call deacons distribute the bread and wine and water over which the Eucharist has been spoken, to each of those present; they also carry them to those who are absent."[30] This is the first clear reference to the liturgical functions of the deacon.

Tertullian of Carthage

Tertullian (ca. 160–ca. 225) was brought up in Carthage as a pagan. He was very well educated, may have been a lawyer, and is the first of the church fathers to write in Latin. One author describes Tertullian in these somewhat off-putting terms: "His dour outlook could not find enduring satisfaction in the church. He needed a system which made of asceticism not a counsel but a precept."[31] This strict attitude eventually took him from the Catholic Church to the fold of the Montanists, a sect marked by asceticism. Tertullian wanted a true church, a pure church, filled with the Holy Spirit and of Spirit-led men.[32]

In the first book ever devoted to baptism as a discrete subject, *On Baptism* (ca. 200), Tertullian provides us with information concerning deacons in his hometown of Carthage:

> Of giving it [baptism], the chief priest [who is the bishop] has the right: in the next place, the presbyters and deacons, yet not without the bishop's authority, on account of the honor of the church, which being preserved, peace is preserved. Beside these, even laymen have the right....But how much more is the rule of reverence and modesty incumbent on laymen—seeing that these powers belong to their superior—lest they assume to themselves the specific function of the bishop![33]

Concerned with the unity and well-being of the church, Tertullian gives emphasis appropriately to the bishop when it comes to the celebration of baptism. After the bishop, however, presbyters and deacons may baptize, but only with the bishop's authority, and, when it is absolutely necessary, even a layman may baptize.

Didascalia Apostolorum

Writing about the year 220, the author of the *Didascalia Apostolorum* (The Teaching of the Twelve Holy Apostles and Disciples of Our Savior) was probably a bishop, who may have been a medical doctor and who may have converted from Judaism. He would have been no friend of Tertullian because he entertains somewhat lenient views about moral issues, permitting repentant sinners to come back to the communion of the church. As Frank Cross puts it, "He is evidently out of sympathy with all rigoristic tendencies."[34]

The anonymous author-bishop is very clear about the role of the bishop and the role of the deacon in relation to each other: "And let [the deacon] be ready to obey and submit himself to the command of the bishop. And let him labor and toil in every place whither he is sent to minister or to speak of some matter to anyone. For it behooves each one to know his office and be diligent in executing it. And be you [bishop and deacon] of one counsel and of one purpose, and one soul dwelling in two bodies."[35]

The deacon is "the bishop's ear, mouth, heart and soul" (II.44.4). After the bishop himself, the deacon seems to have been the most influential and central figure in the local church. His influence extended beyond that of the presbyters. Paul McPartlan writes of the rivalry between deacons and presbyters: "Although it is disedifying in one way to discover this, I think it is also very encouraging in another. Today's problems are rarely completely new."[36]

The *Didascalia* provides us with the lengthiest description of deaconesses in the early church; one description comes in chapter 9 and the other in chapter 16 of the document. In chapter 9 we read:

[The bishop] is the minister of the word and the mediator; and for you he is a doctor as well as your father in God: he gave you birth through water....He is to be honored by you as is God himself, because, for you, the bishop stands in the place of the All-powerful God. The deacon stands in the place of Christ and you should love him. The deaconess should be honored by you as the Holy Spirit is honored. Priests ought to be considered by you as the apostles would be considered, and widows and orphans should be esteemed by you as you would esteem the altar of God.[37]

The author compares the bishop to God the Father, the deacon to Jesus Christ, the deaconess to the Holy Spirit, the presbyters to the apostles, and widows and orphans to the altar of God. The comparison is a little strange to us, but we have already met the comparison of the deacon with Christ and the presbyters with the apostles before in the letters of Ignatius of Antioch. Churches looked after widows and orphans, and their responsibility was to pray for the church. Hence, their comparison to the altar of God. But the deaconess is compared to the Holy Spirit. It may be because the word "spirit" in Semitic languages is a feminine noun, and therefore, seemed readily to suggest the feminine order of deaconesses.[38]

Chapter 16 gives a much longer treatment:

This is why, O bishop, you must take to yourself workers for justice, helpers who will cooperate with you in guiding others towards life. Those among the people who most please you in this respect should be chosen and instituted as deacons: on the one hand, a man for the administration of the many necessary tasks; on the other hand, a woman for ministry among the women. For there are houses where you may not send deacons, on account of the pagans, but to which you may send deaconesses. And also because the service of a deaconess is required in many other domains. In the first place, when women go down into the water, it is necessary that those going down into the water be anointed with the oil of unction by a deaconess. Where no other woman is present, especially where no deaconess is present, it will then be necessary that the one who is conducting the baptism must anoint the woman being baptized, but they should then be anointed only on their heads. But where another woman is present, especially a deaconess, it is not good for women to be viewed by men....Afterward, whether you yourself are carrying out the baptisms, or whether you have charged the deacons and priests with that responsibility, a female deacon should anoint the women, as we have already indicated. But a man should recite invocation (epiclesis) over them in the water. When the woman who has been baptized comes up out of the water, the deaconess should receive her and instruct and educate her so that the unbreakable seal of baptism will be preserved in holiness and purity. For these reasons, we assert that the ministry of a female deacon is especially required and urgent.[39]

A number of things emerge here. Deaconesses did not baptize—the bishop did—but assisted at the baptism of women. This was pastorally appropriate since baptism was celebrated without clothing and was accompanied by an anointing all over the body. Clearly, women were best appointed to assist. They also gave post-baptismal instruction to other women. As adult baptism declined after the time of St. Augustine, so the importance of deaconesses diminished.

Were deaconesses ordained? This is a disputed subject. However, it seems to be the case that the *Apostolic Constitutions* provides for a laying on of hands by the bishop (8.19f). Was this an ordination as we should know it? It is impossible to be certain. The scholars are divided, the evidence is disparate and fragmentary. Aimé George Martimort says "No," while Cipriano Vagaggini, O.S.B., says "Yes." Martimort examines the evidence most thoroughly and I find him persuasive on the issue. Vagaggini overlooks important issues to some extent and then concludes: "The diaconal ministry of the Church had two branches: a masculine ministry and a feminine one for ministering to women specifically."[40] Perhaps the most telling piece of counter-evidence posited by Martimort has to do with the fact that "deaconesses were never given grounds to hope, as were deacons, that they might aspire to a higher degree of ministry."[41]

Hippolytus of Rome, *The Apostolic Tradition*

Hippolytus (ca. 170–ca. 236) was the most important third-century theologian of the Roman Church. A staunch conservative in thought and practice, he was immensely learned, and the great

Origen of Alexandria attended one of his sermons when he visited Rome about 212. Hippolytus's book *The Apostolic Tradition* gives us a wonderful window into the Roman community of his time. The book provides us with the earliest ordination rites that we possess. During the rite, the bishop alone lays hands on the deacon at ordination because "he is not ordained to the priesthood but to serve the bishop and to fulfill the bishop's command....He has no part in the council of the clergy....He does not receive that Spirit which the presbytery possesses."[42] The prayer of ordination is particularly beautiful:

> God, who created all things and ordered them by your Word, Father of our Lord Jesus Christ, whom you sent to serve your will and make known to us your desire, give the Holy Spirit of grace and caring and diligence to this your servant whom you have chosen to serve your church and to present in your holy of holies that which is offered to you by your appointed high priest to the glory of your name; that, serving blamelessly and purely, he may attain a rank of a higher order, and praise and glorify you through your Son Jesus Christ our Lord; through whom be glory and power and praise to you, with the Holy Spirit, now and always and to the ages of ages. Amen.[43]

The passage tells us two important things about the deacon at the time: God the Father has taken the initiative in choosing the diaconal candidate for service in the church, and the deacon is understood as responding to this grace.

One of the deacon's liturgical roles is to present to the bishop (the high priest) the offerings of the faithful during the celebration of the Eucharist. If enough presbyters were not present at the Eucharist, the deacon could assist in the distribution of the cup, maintains Hippolytus.[44] The deacon also played a central role in the celebration of baptism. Hippolytus tells us that deacons held the vessels containing the holy oils used in the ritual.[45] The deacon also accompanied the baptismal candidate down into the water (21.11), and in cases of necessity, as in Tertullian, the deacon could baptize (26.14).

The Deacon and the *Agape* Meal

Agape is one of the Greek words for "love." The *agape* meal was a special religious meal celebrated by the community in order to meet the needs of the poor, the widows, and the orphans, who depended upon the community for the basics of life. In all probability this meal was not originally separate from the Eucharist, for example, the practices described by St. Paul in 1 Corinthians 11 may well refer to the conjunction of what later became separate. The reasons for the separation are not completely clear, but may have had to do with two issues: various abuses that occurred during the celebration (again St. Paul in 1 Corinthians 11 may be alluding to them), and Roman imperial rescripts that forbade the meals of secret societies, social gatherings that had the capacity to foment social and political unrest in the community at large.

In Justin Martyr's description of the Eucharist in his first *Apology* (65–67), the regular community Eucharist seems to have absorbed the fraternal functions of the *agape* meal. Participants deposit foodstuffs and other basics of life with the bishop to be distributed after the liturgy. Yet some decades later in Rome we seem to find the Eucharist and the *agape* meal as distinct. Hippolytus in the *Apostolic Tradition* talks about the *agape* for widows.[46] The bishop was the normal presider, but in his absence a presbyter or a deacon could preside at the *agape*. All present would receive a piece of bread blessed by whomever the presider was, this blessed bread being quite distinct from the Eucharist. The meal was accompanied by prayers, readings from Holy Scripture and the singing of hymns, and when it was over, the distribution of goods to the poor took place, supervised by a presbyter or a deacon.[47] There is general scholarly agreement that by the mid-third century the *agape* and the Eucharist have gone their separate ways.

Cyprian of Carthage

The first systemic and global persecution of the church took place under the Roman Emperor Decius while Cyprian was bishop of Carthage (248–258). From Cyprian's writings we get quite a full profile of the diaconal role. For example, he describes the difficult situation of a young girl who was reluctant to receive communion, but was compelled to by a deacon:

> When, however, the solemnities were finished, and the deacon began to offer the cup to those present, and when, as the rest received it, its turn approached, the little child by the instinct of the divine majesty, turned away its face, compressed its mouth with resisting lips and refused the cup. Still the deacon persisted and, although against her efforts, forced on her some of the sacrament of the cup.[48]

Cyprian clearly does not approve.

In the persecution at Carthage, those who committed the grave sin of apostasy had to be formally reconciled to the church through the *exomologesis* or public penance. However, the circumstances of the persecution were such that sometimes there was no time or opportunity for recourse to the public penance, and in this context Cyprian permitted his deacons and presbyters to "hear confessions," as we might say.

> They who have received certificates from the martyrs, and may be assisted by their privilege with God, if they should be seized by any misfortune and peril of sickness, should, without waiting for my presence, before any presbyter who might be present, or if a presbyter should not be found and death becomes imminent, before even a deacon, be able to make confession of their sins, that, with the imposition of hands upon them for repentance, they should come to the Lord with the peace which the martyrs have desired, by their letter to us, be granted to them.[49]

While Echlin comments appropriately, "The great Cyprian did not feel constrained in his use of deacons by the functions deacons had performed in other ages with other needs," there is no later evidence of such a practice.[50]

During the Decian persecution, many Christians were in prison in Carthage. The community's eagerness to furnish their suffering sisters and brothers with the Eucharist caused a problem. So many were visiting the prison for this purpose, Cyprian was afraid that this would invite hostile reaction from the authorities. So he directed only one presbyter and one deacon to go at a time, and a different pair was to go the next time.[51]

Cyprian took his deacons to task when it was necessary. In another of his letters we hear of a particular problem:

> We have read, dearest brother, your letter which you sent by Paconius, our brother, asking us and desiring us to write again to you, and say what we thought of those virgins who, after having once determined to continue in their condition, and firmly to maintain their continence, have afterwards been found to have remained in the same bed side by side with men; of whom you say that one is a deacon...you have acted advisedly and with vigor, dearest brother, in excommunicating the deacon who has often abode with a virgin; and moreover, the others who had been used to sleep with virgins.[52]

On another occasion Cyprian denounced the crimes of the deacon Nicostratus who had defrauded the church and the poor.[53]

Paul McPartlan offers a concise and precise summary of the deacon's role in Carthage at the time of Cyprian. "Cyprian's deacons distributed the communion cup, heard confessions *in extremis*, acted as his emissaries to other bishops, administered charity and were occasionally tempted to corruption."[54]

Bishop Cornelius and Bishop Fabian of Rome

We have a description of the clergy at Rome from Bishop Cornelius (251–253). "There are," he writes, "one bishop, forty-six presbyters, seven deacons, seven sub-deacons, forty-two acolytes, fifty-two exorcists, readers and doorkeepers."[55] Bishop Fabian of Rome (235–250) divided the city into seven administrative districts, placing each one under the authority of a deacon. He seems to have been more influenced by the seven reputable men of the Acts of the

Apostles than anything else, because in point of fact Rome had fourteen administrative districts.[56] Thus, while there were some forty-six presbyters in the city of Rome, there were only seven deacons, men of authority and responsibility.

The Councils of Arles and Nicaea

Our information for the early centuries of the church in respect of ministry and liturgy is sorely lacking and incomplete. We certainly do not have a detailed blueprint of the ministry of the deacon. Sir Henry Chadwick, one of the premier scholars of the early church, writes of the deacon: "During the second and third centuries there must have been many occasions when the deacons actually celebrated the Eucharist. This practice was frowned upon and at the Councils of Arles (314) and Nicaea (325) explicitly forbidden."[57] The fact that the practice was forbidden means that it was going on, but we do not know where and to what extent. In all likelihood diaconal celebration of the Eucharist was due to two circumstances: the gradual transition from charismatic to organized and structured leadership in the church, and pressing pastoral need.

Edward Echlin makes two points about these conciliar references.[58] First, nothing whatsoever is said about what today would be called the validity of these diaconal celebrations of the Eucharist. Second, the communities who were served with the Eucharist by such deacons appear to have regarded them as eucharistic in the normal sense of that word. As noted earlier, a complete and detailed picture of every aspect of Christian sacramental celebration eludes us, and we should not read too much into such brief and tantalizing references. But the fact of the matter is that the references are there, and we do need to note them.

Egeria

Egeria was probably a Spanish nun who made a pilgrimage to the Holy Land about 385. She kept a kind of travel diary in which she described, among other things, the various liturgies she attended. Here is her description of the evening service in Jerusalem: When the assembly has finished singing the appointed psalms and antiphons, "one of the deacons makes the normal commemoration of individuals, and each time he mentions a name a large group of boys responds *Kyrie eleison* [in our language, Lord, have mercy]. Their voices are very loud. As soon as the deacon has done his part, the bishop says a prayer and prays the Prayer for All."[59] Probably this refers to the deacon's announcing the individual intentions at the intercessions, with the assembly responding, and with the bishop summing up the intentions in a concluding prayer.

Jerome

In the fourth century the church expanded enormously, and there developed the need for presbyters to look after congregations, rather than just bishops as had largely been the case hitherto. Again, rivalries continued. Jerome pointedly comments: "Although [the presbyter] may be less highly paid than a deacon, he is superior to him in virtue of his priesthood."[60] Interestingly, however, it is Jerome who first provides us with a clear reference to the blessing of the paschal candle by the deacon. A deacon called Praesidius, serving the Church of Piacenza in Northern Italy, asked Jerome about 384 to write the hymn-prayer for the blessing of the paschal candle. The saint actually declines the invitation, but in his letter he witnesses to the fact that this blessing of the candle was part of the deacon's ministry.[61]

The Demise of the Diaconate

During the third century, the more numerous presbyters began to assume increasing administrative and liturgical functions. These were functions that in earlier generations had been attended to by bishops and deacons. Times and pastoral need had changed. For all practical purposes the presbyters became quasi-independent overseers of parishes or districts where they were responsible for liturgy and for the other services the church offered, especially to the poor. This had implications for the diaconate. Paul McPartlan summarizes the development thus: "As the presbyters became 'priests,' regularly presiding at the Eucharist for the first time, so the diaconate declined. Many more presbyters were needed, and many of the erstwhile deacons were ordained to the priesthood, for which the diaconate began to appear simply as a preparation."[62] By the Middle Ages, the diaconate had become more or less a step on the way to the priesthood. This demise of the permanent diaconate is acknowledged by the *Basic Norms* of 1998: "Up to the fifth century the diaconate flourished in the Western Church, but after this period, it experienced, for various reasons, a slow decline which ended in its surviving only as an intermediate stage for candidates preparing for priestly ordination."[63]

The Council of Trent

"It is not often realized that the Council of Trent declared itself to be burning with the desire of restoring the pristine understanding of the ministry of deacons, laudably received in the Church from the time of the apostles."[64] In the debate of 1563, the bishop of Ostuni made the following remarks about the diaconate, showing a concern for a much wider understanding than purely liturgical functions: "I desire the function of the subdeacon and the deacon, diligently collected from the writings of the fathers and decrees of the councils, to be restored and put to use, especially the functions of deacons. The Church has always used [the service of deacons], not only in ministering at the altar, but in baptism, in care of hospitals, of widows, and of suffering persons. Finally all the needs of the people are mediated to the bishop by deacons."[65] This bishop also wanted a longer time period between major orders, "at least three or four years," suggesting, in Edward Echlin's words, "the establishment of a temporary 'permanent' diaconate."[66] In point of fact, one of the three presidents of the Council of Trent was Reginald Pole, an English cardinal who missed election to the papacy by only a single vote. He was also a deacon and remained such until he was elevated to the episcopate some time after the Council.[67]

No significant development in the diaconate is to be found for the next three hundred and fifty years or so. The diaconate is simply and normatively a step on the way to priesthood.

From World War II to Vatican II

Discussions among prisoners in the Nazi concentration camp of Dachau led to an interest in promoting the diaconate in the Catholic Church as more than a step towards the priesthood. Two priests, Otto Pies, S.J., and Wilhelm Schamoni, both prisoners at Dachau, promoted the idea of permanent and married deacons. Even while still interned, Schamoni wrote up his notes of their discussions.[68] Later, in 1947, Pies published an article in the Jesuit periodical, *Stimmen der Zeit* (Voices of the Times), reflecting the Dachau conversations exploring the idea of a married diaconate. Pies and Schamoni were supported in this by Josef Hornef, a magistrate, who published in 1948 an article entitled "On the Restoration of the Diaconate." Other published essays on the topic were published, and, gradually, in the post-war years, a movement began in Germany to restore the permanent diaconate. Other contributions to the discussion appeared in the developing countries of Asia and Africa, and so the diaconate become an international issue in the church.

In 1956, the Jesuit theologian Karl Rahner published an essay laying out the theological foundations of a restored diaconate for married men, "Preliminary Dogmatic Remarks for Correctly Framing the Question about the Restoration of the Diaconate." Rahner's contribution to the developing theology of the diaconate was important and led to his promotion of the diaconate at Vatican II.

The deacon in the light of Vatican II has already been discussed. Here we wish simply to note paragraph 29 of *Lumen Gentium* restoring the diaconate, and the 1967 *motu proprio* of Pope Paul VI, *Sacrum Diaconatus Ordinem,* laying the groundwork for the implementation. In the *motu proprio* eleven duties of the permanent deacon are stated, more or less summing up *Lumen Gentium* and *Ad Gentes Divinitus:*

1. To assist the bishop and the presbyters in the liturgy
2. To administer baptism solemnly
3. To be custodian of the Eucharist, to carry Viaticum to the dying, and to give the eucharistic blessing of Benediction
4. To preside at marriages

5. To administer sacramentals and to preside at funerals
6. To proclaim the gospel liturgically and to preach
7. To preside at the Liturgy of the Hours
8. To direct the liturgy of the word
9. To fulfill the obligations of charity and administration
10. To guide scattered Christian communities
11. To promote and support the lay apostolate

In these eleven responsibilities, the traditional duties of the diaconate are represented: ministry of the word, of liturgy, and of charity, or ministry at the three tables of the Word, of the Eucharist, and of charity.

Deacons for Deacons: Lawrence of Rome, Ephrem of Nisibis, Francis of Assisi, and Nicholas Ferrar

The deacon's duty and office is this: that he is entrusted with Christ's ministry to his people. Not the ministry of Christ the Shepherd, the priest or the Lord; but the ministry of Christ the Servant of us all.[1]

The Letter to the Hebrews tells us that "We are surrounded by so great a cloud of witnesses" (Heb 12:1). It is certainly true that the history of the church throws up many witnesses for deacons, men whose lives have exemplified various aspects of diaconate in the highest degree. If today's deacon is entrusted with the ministry of Christ, the Servant/Deacon of us all, light may be thrown on his ministry by having recourse to these stellar examples of diaconate in our Christian tradition. The *Ratio* teaches us that "The ministry of the deacon is characterized by the exercise of the three munera [ministries/offices] proper to the ordained ministry, according to the specific perspective of diakonia," and these are: the ministry of the Word, of the liturgy, and of charity.[2] In this chapter, four deacons are selected whose witness is cherished by the church and whose example is an invitation to deacons today.

Lawrence of Rome (?–258)

Lawrence was one of the seven deacons at Rome under the pontificate of Pope Sixtus II. He was put to death under the Emperor Valerian (253–260) in 258, just four days after the martyrdom of

Pope Sixtus II. Sixtus is believed to have been beheaded along with his four deacons, two of whose names we know, Felicissimus and Agapitus. Some days later, Lawrence was captured and martyred, probably also by beheading, although, according to the received tradition, Lawrence was put to death roasted on a gridiron.[3]

After the Edict of Toleration, the Emperor Constantine, about 330, had a church built above Lawrence's tomb in a catacomb. This tomb became a very popular place of pilgrimage. It was a relatively small church, with stairs providing access down to Lawrence's final resting place in the catacomb. Due to the increasing popularity of the saint, Constantine then built a large basilica on the summit of the hill where Lawrence was buried. Later Pope Pelagius II, finding Constantine's original church in a state of total disrepair, tore it down and reconstructed a new basilica at the level of Lawrence's tomb itself. Finally Pope Honorius III made these two buildings into one, thus establishing the Basilica of San Lorenzo much as it is to this day.

Pictures of St. Lawrence were found on gold goblets discovered in the catacombs, and a church was dedicated to him by Pope Damasus *inside* the walls of Rome, the church on his grave-site being *outside* the city, as was the custom with Roman cemeteries. These buildings demonstrate Lawrence's popularity with Roman Christians. "In fact, no saint, except Saints Peter and Paul, was more honored by the people of Rome from the time of Constantine on."[4]

Lawrence's memory was preserved, however, not only in church buildings, but also in a number of patristic texts: Cyprian of Carthage, Letter 80; Ambrose of Milan, *On the Duties of the Clergy;* and Prudentius, *Peristephanon.* Here we will look at Ambrose and Prudentius.

In his *On the Duties of the Clergy* (Book 1, ch. 41.214–215; Book II, ch. 28.140–141), probably composed about 391, St. Ambrose, Bishop of Milan, commends Lawrence as an example to his clergy. According to the testimony of Ambrose, the prefect of Rome asked Lawrence to reveal the whereabouts of the treasures of the church. So, Lawrence brought together the poor and the sick and said, "These are the treasures of the Church." The poor, and indeed all the people, are the treasures of the church because, in Lawrence's terms, Christ lives in them; according to Matthew 25:31–46, Christ is identified with the hungry, the thirsty, and the poor.

Prudentius, a Spaniard and the greatest of the Latin Christian poets, composed the *Peristephanon*, fourteen hymns on selected martyrs. Of these martyrs, five were deacons: Vincent of Saragossa, who died in 304 and who often preached for his bishop, Valerian, who suffered from a severe stutter; Augurius and Eulogius of Tarragona; Romanus of Caesarea, martyred at Antioch about 304; and Lawrence of Rome. No doubt when Prudentius visited Rome, he took part in the celebration of the Feast of St. Lawrence and visited the basilica dedicated to him. In this poem Lawrence is presented as the New Augustus, who will be the leader of the spiritual Rome, the heavenly Rome.[5]

The popularity of Lawrence among the Romans and the many legends that gathered about him inspired Prudentius to compose his hymn. The hymn picks up the notion that the Christians had amassed a fortune in silver and gold, stowed away in secret vaults. The prefect was overjoyed at Lawrence's willingness to reveal the church's treasures and gave him three days to prepare.

According to Prudentius:

[Lawrence] hastens through the city streets,
And in three days he gathers up
The poor and the sick, a mighty throng
Of all in need of kindly alms.
He sought in every public square
The needy who were wont to be
Fed from the stores of Mother Church,
And he as steward knew them well.[6]

Prudentius knew that the deacon had as one of his roles the dispensing of alms to those Christians in need. The deacon was the steward who knew the poor well and who looked after them. Here was a truly incarnational theology at work. Christ lived in and through these actual people, in all their concrete circumstances. As Prudentius has it, the prefect:

Would behold them clothed in rags,
Their nostrils dripping mucus foul,

Their beards with spittle all defiled,
Their purblind eyes made blear with rheum.[7]

These very ordinary people, in their straitened, undesirable circumstances are Corpus Christi, the Body of Christ, the treasures of the church.

It is no wonder that Lawrence became so popular. This deacon knew well that what really counted was people. People, human relationships, and caring are the real treasures of the church. That is what his martyrdom was about. That is what assured his memorial in the Roman Canon of the Mass. Lawrence in his ministry of charity is a deacon for deacons.

Ephrem of Nisibis (ca. 306–373)

Ephrem was born around 306 in or near Nisibis, probably to Christian parents. He was ordained a deacon by Bishop James of Nisibis. When the Roman Empire had to cede his hometown of Nisibis to the Persians in 363, Ephrem went with most of the Christian community to Edessa in what is today southeast Turkey. In Edessa, which was within the boundaries of the Roman Empire, the exiled Christian community found refuge and a place of safety. There Ephrem established a school of biblical and theological studies. He composed hymns, homilies, and commentaries on Holy Scripture. Many of his writings had an explicitly liturgical setting. We are told by St. Jerome that in some churches Ephrem's compositions were recited after the scriptural lessons in the liturgy.[8] He was also interested in women's choirs, something of a novelty at the time. A deacon, he died ministering to victims of the plague in Edessa in 373.

Ephrem wrote theology in the form of poetry, in Syriac, a dialect of Aramaic, very close to the language our Lord himself spoke. Some scholars insist that Ephrem's Syriac verse is so involved and intricate that the only satisfying way of studying him is in the Syriac language.[9] While that is unquestionably desirable, we are nonetheless well served by contemporary translations, especially those of Sebastian Brock of Oxford and Kathleen McVey of Princeton.[10]

Although a father and doctor of the church, Ephrem is much less well known than others. There are at least two reasons for this. First, his use of Syriac has traditionally made him much less accessible to Western readers unacquainted with the language. However, this in no way means that Ephrem and his Syriac-writing colleagues are less valuable in Christian theology. Sebastian Brock writes: "If these oriental fathers are very little known to Western Christians, this is not due to any intrinsic inferiority on their part, but to the heavily Eurocentric character of the academic study of church history and doctrine."[11] Second, that Ephrem was essentially a poet renders him somewhat suspect, even though he was "the greatest poet of the patristic age, and perhaps the only theologian-poet to rank beside Dante."[12] Regrettably, Western analytic and systematic thinkers have not tended to take with great seriousness those whose theological vision is mediated through poetry. Preference tends to be given to architectonic systematic theologies in which philosophy is often given the dominant role in the shaping of theology.

A major and perduring theme in Ephrem's theological poetry is the inaccessibility of the divine to human reason. That God exists is knowable, but the nature of God remains impenetrable to human intelligence:

> Thousand thousands stand, and ten thousand
> thousands haste.
> The thousands and ten thousands cannot search
> out the One:
> For all of them stand in silence and serve.
> He has no heir of his throne, save the Son who
> is of him.
> In the midst of silence is the enquiry into him,
> when the watchers [angels] come to
> search him out.
> They attain to silence and are stayed.[13]

God's throne in heaven is surrounded by countless ministering angels, standing and serving him. They stand in silence, however, because no one can penetrate the reality of God. God is always more and other. The only heir the Father has "is of him," reflecting the Nicene doctrine of "one in being with the Father." Only in the reverent silence adoring the Mystery of God may one rightly pursue understanding of God. This is a strong theme in Ephrem:

> If then our knowledge cannot even achieve
> a knowledge of itself, how does it dare
> investigate the birth of him who knows
> all things? How can the servant, who
> does not properly know himself, pry into the
> nature of his Master?[14]

What an insight! The servant, that is the human being, lacks any real and substantial self-knowledge, but pries into the reality of God. Ephrem views theology not so much as "faith seeking understanding," because he is all too aware of the fragility of real understanding, but as "faith adoring the mystery," reaching out through limited understanding to adoring in silence the Mystery God is.[15] Ephrem implies that real knowledge of self is the prerequisite for any knowledge of God. If real knowledge of God is sought, it will be found in God's revelation of himself in the person of Jesus:

> If anyone seeks your hidden nature,
> behold it is in heaven in the great womb
> of Divinity. And if anyone seeks
> Your revealed body, behold it rests and looks out
> From the small womb of Mary![16]

If the hidden and transcendent nature of God is hidden in Godself, "in the great womb of Divinity," it is nonetheless revealed and made manifest in the incarnation, "from the small womb of Mary." Here Ephrem bends the normal lines of thought to speak of the Father having a womb, and points to the wondrous paradox of the incarnation by contrasting that "great womb" with the "small womb" of our Lady. Talking about the womb of the Father is a glorious image and much loved by Ephrem. He gives expression to the same theme in the following passage, but this time encompassing the immanence as well as the transcendence of God:

> The Power that governs all dwelt in a small womb.
> While dwelling there, he was holding the reins of the universe.

His parent was ready for his will to be fulfilled.
The heavens and all the creation were filled by him.
The Sun entered the womb, and in the height and depth his
    rays were dwelling.
He dwelt in the vast wombs of all creation.
They were too small to contain the greatness of the Firstborn.
How indeed did that small womb of Mary suffice for him?
It is a wonder if anything sufficed for him.
Of all the wombs that contained him, one womb sufficed:
The womb of the Great One who begot him.[17]

Here the Son is from the "great womb of the Father," born of
the "small womb" of Mary, but he is also found in "the vast wombs
of creation." All things came to be through him and without him
was made nothing that was made. Nowhere, no womb of creation,
is absent of the presence of the Son, who is the medium of creation,
making a christic impress on all that is.

It is in the Eucharist that Christ comes closest to us. For the
Eucharist Ephrem also has many beautiful things to say. My
favorite passage is this:

Christ's body has newly been mingled with our bodies,
His blood too has been poured out into our veins,
His voice is in our ears,
His brightness in our eyes.
In his compassion the whole of him has been mingled
In with the whole of us.[18]

This is a powerful and early representation of the transformation the Eucharist effects in us. Christ is mingled with us through
the Eucharist. His transforming presence, poured into us, transforms us from within, so that his voice resounds in our ears, and his
brightness in our eyes. One is reminded of the frequently quoted
line of St. Teresa of Avila, "Christ has no body now but yours."
Ephrem knew that.

Ephrem teaches modern deacons the importance of words
and images, especially as they are involved in homilies. The craft
of word-weaving is all important and essential to a deacon.
Ephrem exemplifies this to a high degree. He loved words and

images and was a true "philologist," a "lover of words." The English systematic theologian Nicholas Lash describes something of the philology or word-care that should mark all Christians, but especially those who are particularly entrusted with the *diakonia*/ministry of the word. "Commissioned as ministers of God's redemptive word, we are required in politics and in private, in work and play, in commerce and scholarship, to practice and foster that philosophy, that word-caring, that meticulous and conscientious concern for the quality of conversation and the truthfulness of memory, which is the first casualty of sin. The Church, accordingly, is or should be a school of philology, an academy of word-care."[19] If the whole church is made up of those who love the Word and are concerned about the theological veracity of words, how much more the deacon, who is given in *Lumen Gentium* §29 a specific ministry of the word.

Walter J. Burghardt, S.J., one of the premier homilists in the country writes: "To me, the unprepared homilist is a menace. I do not minimize divine inspiration. I simply suggest it is rarely allotted to the lazy."[20] It is clear that Ephrem was inspired, not in the same sense as Scripture, of course, but through his dedication to communicate as finely and as beautifully as possible the gracious attractiveness of God's word/Word. When one begins to think of what must have gone into his preparation of these liturgical poems and homilies that constitute his work, one recognizes in Ephrem a powerful model for deacons in this regard. Ephrem, in his ministry of the word, is a deacon for deacons.

Francis of Assisi (1181–1226)

"Of all the saints, the one whom most people find most Christlike is St. Francis. And I think it is significant that he was never a priest. He was an ordained deacon, a servant, to the end of his life."[21] That historically seems to be the absolute truth, but the only piece of evidence we have of Francis's diaconate comes from Thomas of Celano's account of Christmas Mass at Greccio in 1223. The exact date of Francis's ordination is unknown. But at the Christmas midnight Mass in 1223, he chose to be deacon. The liturgy was celebrated close to the crib, with its manger and straw, its ox and its ass, required by tradition. Then Francis sang the Gospel with his "strong, sweet and clear" voice, according to Thomas of Celano, his biographer.[22] Here is how Michael Robson, O.F.M.Conv., a recent biographer of Francis, describes the event: "Greccio became a new Bethlehem. Just as some medieval theologians depicted sin as something that disturbed the created order, so the liturgical celebration at Greccio had cosmic ramifications....The whole night resounded with harmony and the note of rejoicing....The scene was one of religious fervour which momentarily restored the harmony of creation and the outpouring of God's gifts."[23]

Our emphasis here will be to view Deacon Francis's entire life and ministry as diaconal, and, in particular, his humor (his "holy folly") and his love for God's creation.

Francis's parents were Pietro Bernadone, a wealthy textile merchant, and Pica, of a distinguished French family. The young Francis's wealth and *joie-de-vivre* made him the leader of Assisi's youth. Caught in the intercity feuding between Assisi and nearby Perugia, he was imprisoned (1202–1203). Serious illness at this time brought about a conversion experience. He heard a voice from the cross of San Damiano, broke off relations with his father, and renounced his considerable familial wealth. It is on this famous occasion that we begin to find Francis in his role of "holy fool." He stripped himself naked, returned all his possessions to his father, and embarked on what everyone must have thought was a very foolish road indeed. In his remarkable book *Perfect Fools,* John Saward tells us: "Much that is distinctive in the life of St. Francis corresponds to the spirituality of the fools for Christ's sake. In him we find all the elements of holy folly."[24]

Followers joined him, and he received oral approval for his rule by Pope Innocent III about 1210. The Portiuncula chapel near Assisi became the cradle of the new order. Francis's friend Clare was invested there in 1212, and so the Second Order was founded. The preaching of Francis and his friars initiated in Italy a strong penitential movement among the laity and this developed into the Third Order. The call to poverty of this penitential movement was so extreme, it not only appeared to be sheer folly to many of Francis's contemporaries, but it also created suspicion, trouble, and dissent for the Franciscans for several generations.[25]

Another striking aspect of Francis's holy folly was his missionary zeal. In 1219 during the Fifth Crusade, his zeal took him to the Middle East where he tried in vain to convert the Sultan of Egypt, Malik al-Kamil. That seemed extraordinarily foolish to his peers. By all accounts the sultan treated the holy man with courtesy and sent him back to the crusaders' camp.[26]

Francis's folly found expression in domestic missionary work too. "Francis and Brother Ruffino on one occasion preached naked and were mocked by the people who thought they had gone mad out of an excess of penance."[27] When Francis went on to speak to them of the nakedness and humiliation of Christ, they wept and repented. Folly brought about *metanoia,* change of heart.

Francis's holy folly in these various manifestations brought about in him what can only be called an "inner freedom," a freedom in which there was no stress, no anxiety, because he had cast his cares on the Lord and trusted in him with a joyous abandonment. "The fundamental truth about this simple but fascinating human being is that he was completely filled with God."[28] When you are filled with the truth that is God, you will look strange to other people, as John Saward has it: "In a world gone mad the guardian of truth is invariably dismissed as a raving lunatic."[29]

Francis's love for God's creation finds an excellent summary in the words of Louis K. Dupré: "Who in thirteenth century Italy had a deeper impact upon his culture than Francis of Assisi, an uneducated man, of average intelligence, but a visionary who saw all creation filled with divine life? After him we looked with different eyes at nature, animals, people. We wrote different poetry and we fashioned different paintings. We lived and loved differently."[30] This is no sentimentalism on Dupre's part, but a judgment that could be amply verified historically. Nature poetry, but in relation to God, comes into its own after Francis. In terms of painting, one thinks of the frescoes of Giotto, which had a huge influence on European painting.

Behind these developments stands Francis himself, a man in love with God and with all God's creation. One of Francis's prayers is the short ejaculation, "My God and all things!" To love God is to love God's creation. "When one gives oneself to God, all creation is drawn along."[31] It is out of this deep conjunction of God and creation that Francis was able to pen the canticle "Brother Sun," hymning God's praise through all God's creatures, great and small. It is out of this sense of God's deep presence in creation, especially in the incarnation, that Francis could write of Christmas that it was "the feast of feasts; the day on which God clung to human breasts." "For Francis God could not be sufficiently human and earthly."[32] This is not a quasi-pantheistic reduction of God to his immanence in creation, but a recognition of the consequences of the creation accounts of Genesis, allied to a sense of the cosmic Christ. It is the central Catholic sacramental imagination at work, responding to God's presence everywhere.

Francis's spiritual foolishness for Christ and his consequent sense of inner liberty, his free perspective, and his evangelical and missionary zeal provide a paradigm of inspiration for his fellow deacons. His love of God's creation, full of the divine presence and revealing that presence to those who have eyes to see and ears to hear, shows Francis as a "sacrament of seamlessness," to use Paul McPartlan's phrase, seamlessness between church and world. Francis of Assisi is a deacon for deacons.

Nicholas Ferrar (1592–1637)

Ecumenical awareness and commitment is not an option for a Catholic but a requirement, and especially for the ordained. The *Ratio* states: "The ministry of deacons, in the service of the community of the faithful, should 'collaborate in building up the unity of Christians without prejudice and without inopportune initiatives.' It should cultivate those 'human qualities which make a person acceptable to others, credible, vigilant about his language and his capacity to dialogue, so as to acquire a truly ecumenical attitude.'"[33] It is for this reason that we now turn to an Anglican deacon, Nicholas Ferrar.[34] "Nicholas Ferrar was ordained deacon so as to be able to lead his household's prayers and to be consecrated to the service of his Lord. But he would not be a priest."[35] This is the all-too-brief description given by Bishop Mark Santer in a homily on the diaconate. Ferrar will be little known to most Catholics, but he too is a deacon for deacons.

He was born in London in 1592, the son of a well-to-do merchant, a friend of Sir Francis Drake and Sir Walter Raleigh, and of a pious and devoted Christian mother. Ferrar's London was the London of Shakespeare: beautiful, yet overcrowded, and in places marked by squalor, a breeding ground for the plague. Reputedly he knew the Psalter by heart as a young boy, as well as entire chapters of the New Testament, and the Scriptures were to remain absolutely central to his spiritual life. He was educated at Clare Hall, the University of Cambridge, where he was regarded as one of the most brilliant students of his generation, the main subject of his study being "physic" or medicine. One biographer points out that Ferrar needed both "all his own medical knowledge" as well as his family's care, due to the poor state of his health.[36] He was said to suffer from "ague," a malaria-like fever marked by shaking and quivering and sweating fits.

For this reason he left Cambridge in 1613 and traveled abroad, visiting Germany, Italy, and Spain. During his travels, he almost certainly came across St. Francis de Sales's book *Introduction to the Devout Life,* first published in 1608. "We can be certain that Nicholas knew it and came to love it, for it was one of the many books bound by the sisters at Little Gidding," his religious community.[37] After his return to England in 1618, he went into business for a while, following in the footsteps of his father and brother. He then entered parliament, "but the somber political prospect as well as his religious aspirations determined him to give up the brilliant career which was opening before him."[38] Apparently, a very fashionable London heiress was being promoted as a suitable wife for Ferrar, but he declined, determined to lead a life of dedicated celibacy.

In 1625 Ferrar settled at Little Gidding in Huntingdonshire, an estate purchased by his mother the previous year. Members of his family, including his mother and the families of his brother and sister, joined him there, and they established a sort of religious community. The community numbered about thirty in all. He was ordained a deacon by William Laud, then Bishop of St. David's, in Westminster Abbey on Trinity Sunday, 1626. He never wished to become a priest, probably out of a combination of personal humility and a desire simply to serve his community at Little Gidding in their daily prayer. On the day of his ordination to the diaconate, he wrote out on a sheet of vellum a vow to serve God "in this holy calling, the office of a deacon."[39]

The church at Little Gidding was in very poor condition when the community first became established, and it was a priority for them to put it in good repair as the very center of their lives. Over the west door was an inscription that read, "This is none other than the house of God and the gate of heaven."[40] The Little Gidding community lived a life of devout prayer and worked under a strict rule from 1625 until 1646.[41] Matins and evensong were said in the restored church, but the prayer did not end with those canonical hours. At the beginning of every hour, from 6:00 AM until 8:00 PM, there was an office of fifteen minutes in which groups of the community took their turn. The office consisted of a hymn, a number of psalms, and selections from the Gospels. The *entire* Psalter was recited every day and the Gospels once a month. As well as this, two members kept religious vigil every night from 9:00 PM until 1:00 AM, and during this time again the whole of the Psalter was prayed.

Ferrar's piety and devotion were rooted in the Holy Scriptures and in the Book of Common Prayer. His personal austerity was well known. He himself kept the community vigil two and later three times a week. On the first Sunday of each month and on the major festivals, the Eucharist was celebrated in the church by the vicar of Great Gidding, with Nicholas acting as deacon. They prepared for this celebration with great care and acts of devotion.[42]

As well as their life of prayer, the Little Gidding community was involved in work for the benefit of the whole neighborhood. Three days a week, twenty gallons of gruel, a kind of thin porridge, was prepared for distribution to the poor. The members of the community visited both the poor and the sick, ran a dispensary free of charge for the needy, and offered schooling for the children of the local village. They had a miniature alms-house and offered a permanent home to four poor widows. "Little Gidding was the school, the dispensary and infirmary of the district round about."[43] Ferrar was keen that everyone in the household should know a trade, and so they devoted themselves to bookbinding. For purposes of recreation they had a study circle known as the Little Academy in which they told stories and discussed events of the church's year and Christian virtues.

The "Great Chamber" was the room in which the community assembled for the daily offices. From this room you could look across to the church outside. On one side was an organ to accompany their hymn-singing, and in the center there stood a table on which rested a Bible and the Book of Common Prayer, containing the liturgies of the church. The life of the community revolved around the church and this Great Chamber. It was a life of quiet tranquility and pervasive contemplation, accurately described by Alan Maycock:

> The real background, the primary significance and purpose, of life at Little Gidding was the steady, rhythmic routine of prayer and worship and consecrated effort provided in the daily rule of the household. They knew anxiety of the most urgent kind; they suffered distress and bereavement. Serious crises arose from time to time in their affairs; they were never free from worry about money matters; the most varied activities claimed their attention; and, in spite of all, duties were elaborated and works of charity multiplied as the years went past. But we must never forget that, first and foremost, the life of Little Gidding was the life of Mary, who sat quietly at the feet of Jesus, rather than the life of Martha, who was anxious and busy about many things.[44]

Nicholas was the organizer and administrator, conducting a large correspondence and planning the details of the community's life, yet also spending eighteen out of every twenty-four hours in such a fashion that "his life was a perpetual prayer."[45] When studying, he either kneeled or, like John Henry Newman, stood at a high desk. But it was a well-balanced life, and he constantly recommended to friends that they should lose weight and take frequent exercise, as well as attend to the things of the Spirit. We can truly say that Deacon Ferrar was a minister of the Word, of the altar, and of charity.

In 1633 King Charles I visited Little Gidding and was very favorably impressed with the religious life of the community. A constant visitor to Little Gidding was the poet, scholar, mystic, and man of prayer Richard Crashaw (1612–1649). "He frequently shared the night watches with Nicholas; he found infinite joy in the serenity and regularity of the family's life and worship."[46] Ferrar exercised a considerable influence on another Anglican theologian who was to renounce public life and become a priest. This was the priest-poet-theologian George Herbert (1593–1633). They had become friends at Cambridge, each holding the other in high esteem as "his most entire friend and brother."[47] When Herbert realized he was dying, it was to Nicholas Ferrar that he sent the manuscript of his collection of poems *The Temple* with these words:

> I pray deliver this little book to my dear brother Ferrar and tell him he shall find in it a picture of the many spiritual conflicts that have passed between God and my soul, before I could subject mine to the will of Jesus my Master, in Whose service I have now found perfect freedom; desire him to read it and then, if he think it may turn to the advantage of any dejected poor soul, let it be made public. If not, let him burn it; for I and it are less than the least of God's mercies.[48]

Ferrar was not adverse to burning books and, in fact, on his deathbed gave orders that crates of books he had collected during his travels in Europe were to be burned right away before he died. But not this book of his friend George Herbert. Within three weeks Ferrar had a few copies printed for private circulation, and soon *The Temple* appeared with a preface by himself. The book was to exert "a more profound influence upon religious thought and poetry in England than any other book written during the seventeenth century."[49] Within thirty years of publication *The Temple* had sold 20,000 copies.

Nicholas was a staunch Anglican and held some quite decidedly anti-Catholic views. Thus he considered the Pope the Antichrist and the Mass an abomination. Maycock points out that this was standard opinion at this time of polemics, but adds it is "rather surprising in a man of Nicholas' stamp."[50] On the other hand, the community and especially Nicholas were on very friendly terms with a local Catholic family living near Gidding, and they welcomed a number of Catholic priests from time to time, who spoke of the community in very favorable terms.

The community of Little Gidding raised important socio-political questions in England of the time. With the rising strength of the Puritan movement, the community was attacked as a "Protestant nunnery." But in one of his last conversations with his brother, Ferrar strongly commended the quasi-monasticism that he had established: "It is the right, good old way you are in; keep in it. God will be worshipped in spirit and truth, in soul and in body. He will have both inward love and fear, and outward reverence of body and gesture."[51] Ferrar loved this life and felt it important for his church.

On Sunday, December 3, 1637, Nicholas received communion for the last time, Viaticum from the vicar of Great Gidding, Luke Groose. About three days before his death, he told his community that he wanted to be buried close to the west door of the church. On his deathbed on December 4, 1637, he suddenly rose at the time he was accustomed to take part in the religious vigil, that is 1:00 AM, and exclaimed: "I have been at a feast...at the feast of the Great King," then he sank back quietly on his bed and died.[52] He was buried in the place he himself wanted near the church, and this is how Alan Maycock describes Nicholas's final resting-place:

> He died in his forty-fifth year, almost exactly three centuries ago. In that retired countryside the church of Little Gidding, with a small burial-ground about its walls, stands in the corner of a field, unapproached even by a pathway; and outside the church door is the tomb of Nicholas Ferrar, stripped of every mark of identification....It is impossible today to stand by the bare, simple tombstone...without a profound moving of the heart. Here, in this remote and forgotten place, lies buried one of the most saintly men that has ever adorned the Church of England.[53]

Ferrar and his religious community of Little Gidding were to provide inspiration for the Anglican poet T. S. Eliot in his famous *Four Quartets*. The Anglican Nicholas Ferrar, too, is a deacon for deacons.

Conclusion

Four deacons for deacons: Lawrence of Rome, Ephrem of Nisibis, Francis of Assisi, and Nicholas Ferrar of Little Gidding. Each one of them, but in his own way, is a stellar example of the ministry of the word, of the liturgy, and of charity, as enunciated in the *Ratio*. Each one of them is a light unto our paths and an invitation to similar performance in our lives.

6

Liturgy, the Parish, and the Deacon

The liturgical reform, to the extent it has succeeded, has done so because the vision of the Council Fathers has imbued priests and deacons with its spirit. The liturgical reform, to the extent it has failed, has failed because it has failed to infuse the hearts of priests and deacons with the power of the Sacred Liturgy.[1]

What makes for good liturgy in the parish? Not an easy question to tackle, not least because one's answer is necessarily self-revealing. I am convinced that, while there is no quick-fix formula for good liturgy, there are some basic considerations that can improve our liturgical celebrations, and it is in this context that the revised *General Instruction of the Roman Missal* (G.I.R.M.) is best understood. But, before moving on to these, let's begin with some sad words about the "new" liturgy that emerged after the Second Vatican Council:

> Wherever one goes these days...Catholics seem to be at loggerheads about liturgy. Some dream with nostalgia of the old rite (Pius V, 1570), deploring the all but total disappearance of the Latin language and Gregorian chant; others are irked (now that they have been made conscious of liturgy and the possibility of changing it) either by the manner in which the new rite is performed in their locality or by the failure to reform it much more radically. Some feel they have been arbitrarily bereft of a rite that expressed their experience of God in faith as adequately as anything ever could; while others feel that

they have had imposed on them a compromise rite, bookish and wordy, that doesn't (now they have come to reflect on such matters) embody or direct the very secular and reticent groping for God in the ambiguity of faith which seems their personal experience....But some of the prevailing malaise is surely unnecessary and it seems worth while trying to dissipate it.[2]

These words of Fr. Fergus Kerr, O.P., penned over thirty years ago, could be said to describe our own times. They have a very contemporary ring to them. As the process of liturgical revision continues, not only are Fr. Kerr's words descriptive of the people in the pews, but increasingly also of the community of liturgical scholars and of those who have responsibility for celebrating and leading the rites of the church. They are sad words because the very unifying center of our lives, the liturgy with the Eucharist as its heart, has become divisive and polarizing as Catholics take up different positions and perform the liturgy in sometimes quite strikingly contrasting ways.

Recently, Msgr. Francis Mannion, commenting on the diversity of views among liturgical reformers, has come up with five positions describing the contemporary scene in the United States, but *mutatis mutandis,* his comments hold good also for the attitudes of today's deacons. First are those who advance the official liturgical reform consequent upon the Vatican Council. The other positions stand in relation to this one. Second, and at the traditionalist end of the spectrum, are those who would restore the pre-conciliar liturgy. While there are differences among this group, they all seem to share the basic conviction that the authentic liturgy of the church has been compromised by the Council. Third are the reformers of the reform, who contend that the reform was poorly conceived and poorly implemented: a fresh reform must be initiated. Fourth are the inculturators of the reform; now that all the rites have been thoroughly revised, these people desire the adaptation of the rites to various cultures. Finally come those who advocate a "recatholicising" of the reform. The recatholicising agenda is committed to the following objective: a "vital recreation of the ethos that has traditionally imbued Catholic liturgy at its best—an ethos of beauty, majesty, spiritual profundity and solemnity."[3] What is necessary is not further liturgical change, says this group, but a deeper and richer appropriation of our present liturgy. This particular chapter on liturgy in the parish is closely associated with Mannion's recatholicising of the reform.

The *Constitution on the Liturgy* reads (par. 14): "Mother Church earnestly desires that all the faithful be led to that full, conscious, and active participation in liturgical celebrations which is demanded by the very nature of the liturgy. Such participation by the Christian people...is their right and duty by reason of their baptism."[4]

The *Constitution* continues by insisting that this full and active participation "is the aim to be considered before all else," and that pastors of souls "must zealously strive to achieve it in all their pastoral work." To achieve this, the *sine qua non* is that deacons and priests (not to mention bishops) must be imbued with the spirit and power of the liturgy. As Msgr. Moroney says, this can come about only through prayer: "We do that by prayer: personal prayer, communal prayer, liturgical prayer. We must be men of prayer."[5] Without this presupposition of holiness and our total commitment to its cultivation in our lives as ministers of the church, we will get nowhere in our understanding of the liturgy, either its theology or its performance. A second presupposition is that we give full recognition to what the liturgy *is*. The liturgy is not a human construction to reach God, but is the God-given means of our reaching into or, better, our *being reached* into the life of the divine communion. More colloquially, we do not do liturgy, but God does us in liturgy. "Christ's work was undertaken on behalf of the salvation of the world, and it is this work which liturgists, that is worshippers, perpetuate. Christ is the premier liturgist....Liturgy is not the worship Christians make; liturgy is the religion of Christ perpetuated in Christians. The religion which Jesus enacted in the flesh before the Father is continued in the Church, liturgically."[6]

The *Directory* is no less emphatic on this point, citing Vatican II: "While exercising his ministry, the deacon should maintain a lively awareness that 'every liturgical celebration, because it is an action of Christ the priest and of his body which is the Church, is a sacred action surpassing all others. No other action of the Church can equal its efficacy by the same title and to the same degree.' The liturgy is the source of grace and sanctification."[7] Given that we are striving to be men of prayer, and given that the liturgy is God doing us or making us divine, the following reflections address the question, "How are the faithful to be led to that full, conscious, and active participation?" Another way to say it is this: "What is the requisite pedagogy for achieving such participation?" The answer to the question, the appropriate pedagogy, may be unfolded in five steps:

Step 1: Liturgical literacy is the key without which the sacred mysteries will remain a treasure in a locked room.

In order fully to appreciate any expression of human culture, it is necessary to be inducted into an understanding of what is actually going on. What is not understood is, perforce, ignored.

Leaving aside the particularities of any given example, one hears the constant complaint from teachers at all levels of a pervasive cultural illiteracy. The American writer and educationalist E. D. Hirsch describes the phenomenon of cultural illiteracy in these words:

> Believing that a few direct experiences would suffice to develop the skills that children require, Dewey assumed that early education need not be tied to specific content. He mistook a half-truth for the whole. He placed too much faith in children's ability to learn general skills from a few typical experiences, and too hastily rejected 'the piling up of information.' Only by piling up specific community-based information can children learn to participate in complex cooperative activities with other members of their community.[8]

Hirsch insists that children learn to become skilled and responsible members of society by learning the "stuff" of that society. Absorbing the stories and lore of a tradition and appropriating the ritual gestures of a tradition (initially through constant performance and later through informed intellectual analysis) enables children to take their mature place in society.

Induction into the liturgy takes place in the same way. First, we need to have a basic level of ritual competence through imitative, affiliative repetition. Then, as we grow psychologically and intellectually, we need a proportionate explanation of what these rites mean. That is liturgical literacy. We move from pre-reflective, liturgical performance to reflective and informed liturgical participation. Full, active, and conscious participation in anything comes about through nurture, education, and study. There is nothing magical about liturgical participation; it comes about through gradual and informed exposure to its meaning through various forms of teaching. It is true that the liturgy should not be didactic in any narrow construal of that word. If liturgy is praising the Father, in the Son, through the Spirit, then it is not a classroom lesson. However, without classroom lessons, what people are doing in the praise and worship of God will be so much the less.

There is good precedent for this approach to liturgical literacy in the patristic era, especially the period of the great mystagogical catecheses of the fifth-century fathers. For example, only when the catechumens of the great urban centers of Jerusalem and Milan had been initiated into the church through baptism-anointing-Eucharist by Cyril and Ambrose, were they then formally inducted into the full meaning of the liturgical mysteries. Liturgical literacy, carefully prepared for through scriptural and moral literacy, was the preoccupation of the bishop-catechist during the period of mystagogia (the period after Easter for further penetration of the sacred mysteries).

No one would deny that children need to be prepared for reconciliation, first communion, and confirmation. Liturgical fluency does not end with basic literacy. If fluency is to emerge for the adult active participants in our congregations, then they must learn more about the liturgy. Provision must be made for that learning through marriage preparation programs and infant baptism programs that unpack practice from the liturgical rite, and so forth. It is not so much a matter of creating *de novo* programs of liturgical theology, as much as it is tapping into those key ritual moments that occur in the life cycle and enhancing their appreciation through pastorally sensitive, structured learning.

Step 2: While it is axiomatic that the liturgy is "the source and summit" of the activity of the church, much else needs to happen in the parish.

The center of the liturgy is, of course, the Eucharist, and for most people this celebration occurs on the Lord's Day. Sunday Eucharist is *the* occasion when we are called to experience the liturgy as the source and summit of our lives. However, between one Sunday and the next, the faithful remain a baptized and eucharistic people and are sent out into the world as such. As Paul McPartlan has put it, "The Eucharist not only *gathers* the church, it then *sends us out,* renewed, to gather the world."[9] Gathered, re-affirmed, and restored as Body of Christ in and through the Eucharist, we are called to act as that Body in our world. The world is gathered through the mediated immediacy of our gathering. In eucharistic mission, we are to have the mind and so also the actions of Christ, as those are summarized by him in the synagogue at Nazareth: to bring good news to the poor and afflicted, to proclaim liberty to captives, to give sight to the blind, to lift the burdens of oppression (Luke 4:18ff.). Caring for others, healing the sick, *bringing* good news to the poor by *being* good news to and among the poor are the means by which we, under grace, gather the world.

In practical terms, this gathering of the world will involve parochial plans to enable justice to flourish in our communities. Programs of voluntary action for justice and charitable outreach are demanded by the Eucharist as its moral face in the world.[10] Our eucharistic attitudes need to go beyond the somewhat safe place of "work for justice" to embrace *everything*. We leave Mass to embody in our entire lives—in our families, homes, with our spouses and children, in places of employment and work, in recreation and fun, on the highway—the One whose Body we have eaten. In short, the celebration of Eucharist cannot be the source and summit of our lives if our lives themselves are not striving to be eucharistic in all our contextual circumstances and situations.

Step 3: Take care of the details of the liturgy because God is to be encountered in the details.

The *Constitution on the Liturgy* (par. 34) notes that "The rites should be distinguished by a noble simplicity...." The real challenge is to know in what simplicity consists. "Simplicity" is not a value-free term, but comes laden with a host of presuppositions. At the risk of oversimplification, it might be said that in the broad

Christian tradition there are two fundamental models of simplicity, expressing the two fundamental shapes of the Christian imagination: the analogical and the dialectical.[11] From the standpoint of the dialectical imagination, giving emphasis to God's utter transcendence and reflecting principally the Reformation tradition, simplicity may consist in the lack of ornamentation and ritual richness, focusing as it does on the presence of the Word of God. On the other hand, the Catholic analogical imagination enjoys a more expansive appreciation of simplicity, manifesting and celebrating God's presence as radically immanent. Simplicity in this context will not consist in stripping down the liturgy to its most basic, nude, component parts, but rather in the perfect harmonizing of the complex forms and parts of the entire liturgical celebration.

In practice, this will mean considering the details as so many *loci* in which the Mystery of God is to be encountered and engaged. The Spirit-led encounter with Christ, and the location in him before the Father, is impossible without the "flesh and bones" of liturgical detail.

This is the particular care and concern of the various liturgical ministers, for our purposes, especially the deacon: checking that all the liturgical vessels are in place; that books are properly marked; that all liturgical ministers know exactly what to do and how to do it, so that no one gets in the way of the mystagogy. To enable that kind of competent, ministerial choreography means that people need to be taken through their paces by someone who is competent to do so. And again and again, until they have got it right! It is impossible to enter into the prayer of the Easter Vigil, for example, unless everything is in one place and has been attended to ahead of time, especially if one is about to be baptized or received into the church. Mistakes will always happen in liturgical celebrations and are virtually unavoidable, but when they occur due to habitual carelessness, something is fundamentally wrong. While it may be acknowledged that an obsession with details may lead to liturgical monophysitism, this seems not to be in the forefront of sins against the liturgy in our time. Thus the deacon must be a "liturgist" not only through his studies, but in the praxis of the liturgy itself. He must not only love prayer, he must love praying—especially by contributing to the preparation of the Liturgies of the

Word, the Eucharist, and of the Hours. The deacon should not only lead the prayer, but lead others to prayer as well.

Step 4: Liturgy must be predictable for the people to have ownership and to be actively participant.

Liturgy is predictable if it occurs in the same basic pattern with regularity. The comfort level for ritual increases, and so, therefore, the capacity for graceful encounter with God, when people know what to expect, what to say, and what to do.

This is the principle to which David Martin alludes when he affirms that "Norms, standards, formulae, routines...exist to stabilize the molten wax of vision and pass on the imprint."[12] Our prayerful but ill-thought-out changes in the drama of the liturgy are disturbances that affect not only the congregation's comfort and identity. They do more: the abandonment of liturgical stability and predictability also affects our sense of transcendent Mystery. It is as if the flow of the "text" that is the liturgy, interpolated with spontaneous gloss even of a broadly theological nature, is no longer able to induct us into the sense of God. All the constructs of the liturgy intend such a sense, but if they are to work and to be effective, predictability and stability of performance are required. Spontaneity and conviviality certainly have their place at times, but when they intrude upon the predictability of the liturgy they become singularly dysfunctional and disruptive.

Step 5: Deacons are stewards of the mysteries, not liturgical entrepreneurs.

What is required of the deacon, and what the people have a right to expect, is that he celebrates the liturgy according to the mind of the church as that finds expression in the liturgical books. Vatican II's *Constitution on the Sacred Liturgy* is insistent on this point: "Absolutely no other person, not even a priest, may add, remove, or change anything in the liturgy on his own authority."[13] Accepting and performing this charge is proper liturgical style. As with the presbyteral celebrant, the deacon does not have to make up the liturgy as he goes along, does not have to devise new techniques to engage the people, because the liturgical mysteries are not his. They belong to *all* the people of the church. The ministers are stewards of the mysteries. As Anthony Ruff, O.S.B., has written, "While it is appropriate and desirable that each priest celebrates Mass with his own style and personality, it is not appropriate that each priest in effect develop his own rite, as has happened since the Council."[14] Being the man you are, with the gifts you have to offer is what is required, and not what has been pejoratively described as "the game-show" approach to liturgical presidency which seems to focus unduly on the priestly or diaconal role. The people (even when entertained) are passive spectators at what might be reduced to a mere priestly or diaconal event. By the same token, when priests or deacons take liberties in changing official texts or improvising on ritual elements, the liturgical rite is destabilized and the people are disenfranchised and marginalized.[15]

Good liturgy and good liturgical presidency aim at letting the rites themselves shape self-understanding and ecclesial understanding, so that that understanding may be passed on to the next generation, and the next after them. That is what stewardship is about. It does not imply a spurious kind of freedom to do whatever one wants with what has been entrusted to one. The *Directory* instructs deacons: "The deacon is to observe faithfully the rubrics of the liturgical books without adding, omitting, or changing of his own volition what they require. Manipulation of the liturgy is tantamount to depriving it of the riches of the mystery of Christ, whom it contains, and may well signify presumption toward what has been established by the Church's wisdom."[16] These are strong words indeed. This is quite different, however, from what has been regarded as "rubricism," an excessive and obsessive concern for the mechanics of the liturgy. The rubrics exist so as to avoid unnecessary distraction. Anthony Ruff, O.S.B., writes: "Quiet and unobtrusive observance of the rubrics is entirely at the service of the prayer of the entire assembly. The laity should not have to adjust to the idiosyncrasies of liturgical ministers every time they attend Mass."[17]

The above five steps mean that the priest and the deacon must be not only men of prayer but also men of obedience. "Obedience to the prayer of the Church, obedience to the Word of God which calls him to die to himself in the model of Christ, and obedience to the euchology and rites he prays."[18] That kind of obedience is not a matter of submitting oneself in a blind fashion to authority and putting one's own liturgical creativity into abeyance. It is more a matter of not getting in the way as God's holy people are led further into the Divine Mystery through the prayerful service of the rites by the deacon and priest.

Let us end this section by drawing attention to some recent words of David N. Power, O.M.I., professor emeritus of liturgy at the Catholic University of America, and no traditionalist when it comes to liturgy: "A key question about how well a priest or deacon functions is whether or not when he prays publicly and turns to God, he draws those present into prayer or simply leaves them listening to him or tuning him out. Obviously, the question is for the people to answer."[19]

The Deacon and the G.I.R.M.

There is a suspicion abroad in some quarters that the issuance of the revised *General Instruction of the Roman Missal* (G.I.R.M.) is clear evidence of the Holy See downgrading lay liturgical participation and emphasizing clerical dominance. This is simply untrue. As Anthony Ruff points out, if one compared the revised G.I.R.M. with its predecessor, one would find that "the revised G.I.R.M. retains *everything* found in its predecessor document concerning active participation of the entire assembly." He goes on to say that if the church authorities were trying to reduce such participation, the revised G.I.R.M. is "a rather weak start and an inept offensive."[20]

Msgr. James Moroney, executive director of the U.S. Bishops' Liturgy Secretariat, addressed the National Association of Diaconate Directors on the deacon and the new G.I.R.M., and it is this address that is the basis for my remarks on this topic.[21] At the outset Moroney made the central point: "Right from the start the definition of 'diakonia' as kenotic self-giving and service at both the table of sacrifice and the table of charity must guide us in our reading of the identity and function of the deacon as envisioned by the latest revision of the Roman Missal."[22] If the deacon serves at the altar, he must serve too in charity among the people of God. He must be the voice of God's people as they articulate their needs before him: "This is why the deacon is the ordinary minister of the 'Kyrie,' all litanies and even the general intercessions....He is, in a very real sense, their voice, both in the liturgy and in the world....The general intercessions are the prototype of diaconal prayer."[23] So, in his seamlessness, his movement from the church to the world and from the world to the church, the deacon is uniquely placed, in virtue of his intimacy with both church and world, to invite the assembly to share the sign of peace, to kneel, and to bow their heads.

Now let us look in a little more detail at some of the instructions governing the role of the deacon—and only the deacon is the concern here—at the celebration of the Eucharist. In laying out these instructions, the actual sequence of the Mass rather than the order of instructions in the G.I.R.M. will be followed.[24]

1. Before the celebration begins, and in view of what is about to take place, an appropriate silence should be observed in the sacristy or vesting area (#45). This helps the deacon to recall just what the divine act of grace is all about, to recollect himself prayerfully before beginning.

2. A deacon wears the alb with a cincture (unless the alb is made to fit without one), the diaconal stole, and a dalmatic (in the color of the liturgical season). If the alb does not cover the ordinary clothing at the neck, the amice should be put on first.

3. If more than one deacon is present, they may distribute among themselves the different parts of the same ministry or duty. For one example, one deacon may take the sung parts while another assists at the altar (#109).

4. The altar is a profound symbol of Jesus Christ and is the most important and central element of liturgical furniture in the church building. When the deacon enters the sanctuary, he salutes the altar with a profound bow and then, with the priest, kisses the altar. If the tabernacle is in the sanctuary, there is a genuflection towards it (#49).

5. A deacon carries the Book of the Gospels, "slightly elevated," in the procession. In this case, the deacon does not bow to the altar. The book is then placed on the altar.

6. The deacon proclaims the Gospel during the Liturgy of the Word, first seeking a blessing from the presider. All other ministers in the sanctuary should turn and face the ambo to show special reverence during the reading of the Gospel.

7. Before reading the Gospel, the deacon greets the people with hands joined saying, "The Lord be with you...." (#134).

8. Occasionally, the deacon may preach the homily: "The homily should ordinarily be given by the priest celebrant....He may entrust it at times to a deacon" (#65).

9. The priest introduces and concludes the General Intercessions, while the individual intentions should be announced by the deacon, or in his absence by another suitable person (#71).

10. The deacon prepares the altar with corporal, purificator, Missal, and chalice (#36)

11. At the presentation of the gifts, the priest receives the gifts and hands them to the deacon who puts them on the altar.

12. During the Eucharistic Prayer, the deacon stands near but slightly behind the priest (or concelebrating priests), so that he can assist with the chalice or the Missal.

13. From the epiclesis, that is immediately after the Sanctus, until the showing of the chalice, the deacon kneels unless health reasons prevent him from doing so.

14. The deacon assists at the showing (elevation) of the chalice at the end of the Eucharistic Prayer.

15. The deacon invites the assembly to share the sign of peace by saying, "Let us offer each other the sign of peace."

16. If the situation calls for it, the deacon may assist the priest in breaking the eucharistic bread (#83).

17. The deacon may help distribute the eucharistic bread into various patens or ciboria for the holy communion of the faithful, and pour the Precious Blood into additional chalices if they are required.

18. The deacon may assist at the distribution of communion, and he is the normal minister of the chalice.

19. The deacon assists in taking the corporal, purificator, chalice, and Missal from the altar after holy communion is over.

20. At the final blessing the deacon invites the assembly to bow their heads to receive God's blessing, and after the blessing dismisses them with the formula provided in the Missal.

Conclusion

In the liturgy God is drawing us into his own very life. The deacon is privileged to serve this divine project, and service is the operative word. We have seen earlier in chapter 2 that the deacon is the *waiter* at God's Table, *not* the host. He proclaims God's Word, *not* his own. He is the unobtrusive servant enabling the liturgy to unfold smoothly to achieve God's purposes. That is what the deacon commits to in his ministry to the altar, and for this reason he should never draw attention to himself but only to the One whom he and, indeed, every Christian serves. But he serves with all the excellence he can command. Perhaps the last word in this chapter on the liturgy and the deacon should go to the *Directory*. There we find, briefly but succinctly, a précis of what the Eucharist should mean and be to a deacon: "Above all, deacons should participate with particular faith at the daily celebration of the Eucharistic sacrifice, possibly exercising their own proper liturgical *munus*/ministry, and adore the Lord, present in the sacrament, because in the Blessed Eucharist they truly encounter Christ who, for love of man, became an expiatory victim, the food of life eternal and friend of all who suffer."[25]

7

The Spirituality
of the Deacon

*Christianity is not real until it has insinuated itself into
the blood and the bones, until it becomes an instinct, as
much physical or spiritual.*[1]

When a deacon is ordained, he does not cease to be a member
of the holy People of God. His life, rather, is contoured to serve that
holy people. His spirituality is that of a Christian, but a Christian
whose very witness as a deacon has a certain publicness about it
that invites him to live the life in Christ more intensely for the sake
of the whole church. The single most important insight for the spiritual life of any Christian, and especially for a public minister of the
church like the deacon, is to view all life and everything in it in deep
union with God. It is to recognize that outside of God there is quite
literally no-thing.

With this backdrop we can appreciate the meaning of Robert
Barron when he makes this bold, clear, and accurate statement of
the raison d'etre of the church: "God...comes relentlessly searching
after us. Because of this questing and self-emptying divine love, we
become friends of God, sharers in the communion on the Trinity.
That is the essence of Christianity; everything else is commentary."[2]
What Barron claims is not novel, but he has a particularly fine way
of bringing to expression the key idea of St. Paul: "[I]t is no longer
I who live, but it is Christ who lives in me" (Gal 2:20). It is the one
fundamental insight that transforms the shape of what it means to
be spiritual. It abandons any extrinsicism and sense of disjunction
between God and the self, between God and creation. Thinking
back to the chapter entitled "Deacons for Deacons," it is a very
Franciscan thing to emphasize.

Who is this God with whom, as church, we are all called to deep union? It is a God whose very being is communion, a communion of Father, Son, and Holy Spirit. It is a thoroughly relational view of God. Let us turn to the Gospel of St. John, chapter 14: "On that day you will know that I am in my Father, and you in me, and I in you" (v. 20). God is this Trinitarian Being as communion into which we humans are invited and brought by grace.[3] The same foundational idea appears in John 17, where the Lord says, "I ask not only on behalf of these, but also on behalf of those who will believe in me through their word, that they may all be one. As you, Father, are in me, and I am in you, may they also be in us, so that the world may believe that you have sent me" (vv. 20–21). The communion with God becomes our communion with God, but also and at the same time our communion with one another: the Father in the Son, the Son in the Father, we in them, and they in us. That is the God with whom as church we are called to deep union. It is, therefore, this relational God, this Divine Being as Communion, that shapes our self-understanding as church—chapter 2 of this book—and our daily spirituality. "Our mission as Church is to be a sign and an agent of the divine relations of mutual, equal and ecstatic love that are at the heart of the universe. The Church is this message. The Church's being is communion. Its very being is mutual relations. The Church is the sacrament of relationships, called to witness to the relational God. This is the grace that the Church is to be for the world."[4]

Intimacy with God

How does a deacon enflesh this spirituality of communion? How does a deacon let this God whose Being is Communion become insinuated into his being and his bones? First, by developing deep intimacy with the Lord Jesus. An acquaintance is not a friend, and a friend is not necessarily deeply intimate with us. What transforms acquaintance into friendship and friendship into deep intimacy is time spent with the other. A deacon needs to spend much time with Jesus. Time spent with Jesus will make all the difference in our lives, not simply in the private and individual parts of our lives, but in the *whole* of our lives. We will become different.

"When Christ comes to dominate our lives, he draws all of our energies—physical, psychological, sexual, emotional, intellectual—around him, pressing them into his service."[5]

Physical, psychological, sexual, emotional, and intellectual energies all say who we are in our daily network of relationships. Letting Christ into our lives through deep intimacy changes the way we are and relate in these dimensions of life. The dimensions take on, as it were, a Christ-shape. We begin, ever so slowly at first, to be absorbed by those words of St. John noted above. The Father is in the Son, and the Son is in the Father, and they are in me, and I am in them. Baptized into the Body of Christ, nourished and fed at the Eucharist, spending ample time in deep intimacy with this Christ whose Body I am—all of this absorbs me in such a fashion that prayer becomes not merely my talking to God—as though I were "outside" God—but my talking in God. Robert Barron writes: "It is this peculiar intimacy—praying in God and not just to him—that gives the Christian practice of prayer its unique texture."[6] This intimacy in God, emerging from time spent with Jesus, enables us to re-read ourselves, to construct the divine narrative of our lives, and to see life as a unity in the Divine Communion.[7]

It is something of a cliché to acknowledge that we are very busy people. That is so true and obvious that we scarcely need it to be drawn to our attention. It is the negative and destructive fallout from this busy-ness that is our largest danger. "In a culture of busyness it is easy for believers just to give God some slots in the diary and after them to go on to the next thing."[8] This is how we escape from intimacy in and with God. To move into the mode of divine intimacy we should take definite opportunities to pray beyond the scheduled slots of morning and evening prayer, of particular devotions, of the Eucharist, or of whatever our prayer pattern happens to be. We should sometimes pray as long as it takes. We should be very generous with God in terms of our time.

Intimacy comes from prolonged time in the presence of another, becoming integrally aware of the other and of the other's name. My diaconal ordination retreat was conducted by Msgr. Michael Kirkham. He illustrated beautifully the importance of names. He related that he had found his father's diaries after both his parents had passed away. In his father's diary for the year 1918, the year in which his parents had married, his mother is first referred to as Miss Brown. "On January 23rd, I was introduced to Miss Brown. February 1st, Miss Brown and I took a stroll in the woods. February 15th, I attended a musical evening in Preston with Miss Brown. February 21st, I went to Doris's home for tea." Miss Brown becomes Doris. If we are to move from a scheduled professionalism with God to intimacy with Abba/Father, as sons in the Body of Christ, time must be spent in his presence, as long as it takes. Following are some ways of moving into deeper intimacy with the divine: prayer, *lectio divina*, the psalms, pilgrimage, and the sacrament of reconciliation.

Prayer

The first thing to say about prayer is "Just do it!"

Sometimes I get asked, "How do you pray?" On such occasions when people are asking for guidance from me in their prayer life, I know exactly the meaning of those words of the Lord, "Physician, heal thyself." In response, however, to such requests, one needs to emphasize that there is no exact way to pray, a way that is exactly the same for all people. We are different, and so we need to find out what works best for ourselves. One spiritual writer makes the point: "We need doctors, psychiatrists, religious teachers and specialists in every branch of knowledge, and we should be fools if we did not listen to them, but we must never allow any expert to dominate our lives....If we do not meet God within our own inner selves, our religion can degenerate into an idolatry of the institution, or the worship of an ideology, a system of ideas."[9] In that sense, there are no experts in prayer, we just need to do it, but it is possible to offer some reflections from one's experience, however flawed and limited, that may be of help or point in the right direction.

Lectio Divina

Lectio divina, or divine reading, is commended by the *Ratio* as a daily practice: "The candidate must learn to know the Word of God ever more deeply and to seek in it constant nourishment for his spiritual life by means of its loving and thorough study and the daily exercise of *lectio divina.*"[10] Every day, starting small with baby steps as it were, set aside some time for this immensely valuable practice of *lectio divina*/divine reading. It is a spiritual exercise marked by four steps:

1. *Lectio* or reading. This is not speed-reading, but very slow, careful reading, letting the words sink in.
2. *Meditatio* or thinking, thinking about what one has read. This includes asking questions, being intellectually curious about this word or phrase or that, what is behind the words, and so forth.
3. *Oratio* or praying. This is simply opening one's heart and pouring it out to our Father, saying what comes to mind and to our lips. It can take different forms: praise and thanksgiving for benefits and blessings, sorrow and contrition for failure and sin, petition and intercession for the needs of others.
4. *Contemplatio* or silence. After the first three steps, remain silent for some time, permitting no thoughts or ideas to enter one's head. Just be in God's holy presence, listening for the music that is silent.

This practice of divine reading is a transforming experience if practiced regularly. What should we use for our *lectio divina*? Two books are of special significance to a deacon because of his ministry of the altar, the lectionary and the sacramentary. For our *lectio* we could use one of the readings for a given day, perhaps the Old Testament reading. We tend to be so unfamiliar with the Old Testament, and this could open our eyes to its many-sided richness. The sacramentary is the Roman Missal. What about taking the major eucharistic prayers or the prefaces for our divine reading? A careful reading and praying of the sacramentary alerts us to all kinds of wonderful spiritual meaning that might otherwise pass us by because of our sheer familiarity with these prayers. Our ministry at the altar would be singularly enhanced.

One master of *lectio divina*, Michael Casey, O.C.S.O., speaks of the scriptures in this spiritual exercise in the following way, but his meaning could very easily be extended to the liturgical texts of the sacramentary as well: "The Scriptures are not only food, they are also medicine. The experience of compunction during reading is a moment of high intensity that embraces not only the present; it has the capacity to heal the past and to fill us with energy for a more divine future."[11] Not only does divine reading feed our souls with spiritual nourishment now, it also heals us of the spiritual wounds of the past. As memories of failing and falling are recalled, we are filled with God's healing presence, and are enabled to face the present and the future with a renewed sense of God's grace abounding more and more.

The Psalms

"Praying in the name of the Church and for the Church is part of the ministry of the deacon."[12] A deacon commits to praying daily at least the morning and evening prayers from the church's Liturgy of the Hours. The heart of this prayer is the Psalter. The psalms were the Lord's own prayer as a Jew, and, knit into his Body, his prayer becomes ours even as ours becomes, over time, his. Even so, the psalms can be difficult for us to pray, the culture and the presuppositions of the psalmist at times quite alien to our own. What can we do as deacons to pray the psalms more efficaciously?

First, we must recognize that Christian prayer is always a corporate venture. We pray in the name of the entire church, Christ's Body throughout the world, and we make the prayer of intercession for the church and the world. This is particularly important for a deacon who in his very *diakonia* attempts to be a sacrament of seamlessness between church and world. "Intercession is not a separate prelude to diakonia, and diakonia is not only the amen of the prayer of intercession. For intercession is, like other acts of diakonia, a *deed* of participating in a process of giving hope, compassion and justice."[13] While the names of those closest to us in relationship will come to our minds and lips most often at times of prayer, there is a fundamental sense in which, given that we are all knit together as Christ's Body, the names of the entire Body are inscribed on our hearts when we pray. One person is not merely "one" person in the Body of Christ. Where one is, others are; where one prays, others are praying.

A very rich source for exploring the theology and spirituality of the psalms is the work of the late Fr. Carroll Stuhlmueller, C.P. Two essays by Fr. Stuhlmueller and the posthumously edited book *The Spirituality of the Psalms* will repay any deacon's time.[14] The psalms, he tells us, are the very heart of the Bible, are there right in the middle of our Bibles, crafted out of the tenacious memories and prayer patterns of the people of ancient Israel. He recommends seven principles for praying the psalms that seem to me very useful for a deacon:

1. Believe firmly that every day has its own grace; believe and act as though God has a special grace today for the entirety of his creation. This makes us alert to listening for his voice, to seeing his hand at work, flowing from the psalms.

2. Read prayerfully the text of the psalms, slowly and reverently, savoring and enjoying the words, sucking on them as though they were a hard candy. "Read with the faith that God is speaking each word as though for the first time."[15]

3. Read and pray the psalms with imagination. Try to get a sense of what was going on when the psalms were originally crafted and prayed, and enter into this with empathy.

4. Read and pray the psalms according to key words. Certain key words in poetry—and the psalms are absolutely poetry—occur again and again. Be on the lookout for them, see what they have to say about God's message, and hear what they are saying *to you*.

5. Read the psalms with other parallel passages. Often in our Bibles, though not in our office books, the psalms will refer to other passages from the Bible. They can throw light one upon another, as the Bible interprets the Bible, so to speak.

6. Read the psalms according to the liturgy. On special occasions, solemnities and feasts, the psalms are chosen by the church because they seem to speak an appropriate message for this particular liturgical celebration. Stay clued into that message.

7. Consult commentaries to enhance your understanding and knowledge of the Psalter.

Putting some flesh on the bones of Fr. Stuhlmueller's principles for praying the psalms, we could make a commitment that, once a week, as time permits, we will pray morning or evening prayer with a pen or pencil in hand. Underline what strikes you in the psalms, words or phrases that come over with a particular strength or force. For example, on the occasion of the first anniversary of September 11, 2001, Psalm 86 was one of the psalms for morning prayer. Verse 5 leapt off the page for me:

> For you, O Lord, are good
> and forgiving,
> abounding in steadfast love
> to all who call on you.

I found this line of prayer framing my whole day, shaping my thoughts and feelings and attitude.

When the time of prayer is complete, turn to a commentary or study aid and explore further for yourself the meaning of a phrase in the psalm. This is where commentaries come in. One of my many addictions, perhaps stemming from years of studying Hebrew at University College Dublin, is collecting commentaries on the Psalter. The saving grace of this addiction is that the commentaries actually get used. Once a week, sometimes more often, I will turn to Artur Weiser's *The Psalms*.[16] It is out of print now, but worth trying to track down. I have seldom turned to Weiser's commentary for enlightenment and been disappointed. Thus Weiser says that Psalm 86 is an individual lament in which the worshipper cries out to God from his need and pain. And of the verse that so affected me, he says, "From v. 5 onwards, God is recognized as the cause of the answer. This by no means unimportant stylistic form expresses the course which every genuine prayer must take, from lifting up one's soul in search of God to the confidence that comes from having found him."[17]

It takes time to read commentaries, but it is always rewarding. Jotting down in the margins of my office book some notes from my psalm exploration means that next time I pray this particular psalm, the insight is there yet again.

In the final analysis, the most important thing to note about the psalms in our diaconal prayer is our commitment to pray them and to keep at it, when we feel like it and when we do not. This is a key way to developing intimacy in and with the Divine Communion of the Trinity, and to transforming our lives in literally wonder-full ways.

Pilgrimages

It is interesting that in all the higher religions of the world the custom of going on pilgrimage to a holy place has been an important aspect of spirituality. In February 1995, I was serving as deacon at the Cathedral of the Madeleine, Salt Lake City, and I went with the cathedral choir pilgrimage to Rome and Assisi. It was a time of great grace. My mother had died just weeks before. I was a religious professional, a deacon serving full-time in a busy parish, but I was hurting in all kinds of ways. I didn't want to go on this pilgrimage. I was too busy—with parish duties, with my family, with my own grief. Yet I went, and I recall with profound gratitude a sense of overwhelming peace and joy as I preached at the tomb of St. Peter to our small group. I almost couldn't go on. Was it the emotion of the moment in that holy place? Unattended grief being expressed? It would be foolish to deny these, but it would be even more foolish to suggest that the reality of the experience is exhausted simply by acknowledging such reasons. Something more profound was going on, a sense of being overwhelmed by God's holy presence.

Now, we are always in God's holy presence, of course, but we are not always aware of it. Pilgrimage, involving a very real and literal dis-location, being moved out of the comfort and security of our ordinary place in the world, may be just what we need from time to time to find ourselves overwhelmed by God. Pilgrimage does not have to be to exotic and faraway places. The Stations of the Cross are a kind of pilgrimage. In fact, the Stations represent an ordinary form of pilgrimage-dislocation for the majority who can not actually go to Jerusalem to trace the *Via Dolorosa* for themselves. "This devotion probably derived from the practice of fourth century pilgrims in Jerusalem following the street from Pilate's house to Calvary. Wishing to re-enact it when they returned home, they set up a series of pictures or carvings and those who were unable to make the journey overseas could participate with them in an act of piety."[18] A deacon is the ordinary presider at this most popular devotion, especially so during Lent.

The Sacrament of Reconciliation

"When, at the end of his career, the Curé d'Ars was asked what wisdom he had gained about human nature from his many years of hearing confessions, he responded, 'people are much sadder than they seem.'"[19] All of us live with a radical sense of not being fulfilled and satisfied because of things we have said and done and left unsaid and undone, and not just because we have unfulfilled aspirations in life. This is the dysfunction of sin, what Henri de Lubac, S.J., called "this mysterious limp" from which we all suffer.[20] Everyone knows about this limp. Fr. Robert Barron describes the limp most egregiously at work nationally and personally: "Never forgetting, never forgiving, never recovering from past offenses, peoples around the globe allow their lust for vengeance to well up unchecked. And the same phenomenon can be seen in families and communities where grudges are borne for decades, even when the originating offense is long forgotten."[21] All Catholics, but most especially those like deacons who exercise a public ministry in the church, need to avail themselves of the sacrament of reconciliation. We know in our bones our need of it as much as we are aware of its disuse in the church today. Could it be that the lack of holiness in our own lives and in the wider life of the church is in part a consequence of the sacrament's disuse? Barron sadly concludes: "The breakdown in confessional practice has made the church sick by neglect."[22] Every deacon needs to attend to the sickness of his own soul using all the means described in this chapter, and especially this particular sacrament of healing. Further, the deacon must admonish those entrusted to his care to be, in the words of St. Paul, "reconciled to God."

Conclusion

I suspect that most of us in the diaconate community, myself included, would want to shape our lives in Christ around the practices mentioned above. I also suspect that most of us will put off this radical shaping, not out of ill will, but because we are not starting from scratch in the spiritual life. We carry around with us baggage and freight that have come to us from others; we also have baggage of our own making, habits and customs and ways of doing and not doing things, even holy things, that are debilitating and destructive. Our lack of holiness comes both from infection by others and from the ways in which we infect others. As one author puts it: "We are all victims of victims. One of the saddest aspects of the human condition is our apparent inability to stop transmitting crippling neuroses from one generation to another."[23] The wonderful news, however, is that we are not locked into the way we are. We are able to change, albeit with much work and pain, through the "law of the Cross," the Paschal Mystery. By conforming our lives more fully to the Lord through such practices, we move slowly into intimacy with God, and nothing is better.

Diaconal Marriage

One's marriage partner is not a cipher to be decoded but an inscrutable person to be embraced as mystery. ...Marriage is paschal to the core and consequently it is as much about dying as it is about new life.[1]

Self-gift, self-donation to others, is the very essence of the diaconate, and the deacon is called to be the sacrament par excellence of self-donation in his community. If the deacon is married, as the majority of permanent deacons are, he is called first to enflesh this diaconal service to his spouse. His spouse, in turn, is called to enflesh this self-giving to him, so that as a couple their marriage becomes a mutual icon of what the deacon is called to demonstrate in his person.

If we return to the charter of the diaconate in *Lumen Gentium* §29, it is noticeable that little is said of marriage and the diaconate: "With the consent of the Roman Pontiff, this diaconate will be able to be conferred upon men of more mature age, even upon those living in the married state."[2] Nothing more is said. Marriage in relation to the diaconate is both undeveloped and underdeveloped—but perhaps the experience of marriage is the ingredient necessary for such development to occur. And, if the experience of marriage is the necessary ingredient, it also follows that the experience of sexuality is a necessary ingredient. Not only is the theology of marriage underdeveloped in relation to the diaconate, but so also is the concomitant theology of sexuality. Both necessarily go together. Vatican II set the stage for integrating sexuality and marriage by mentioning as on an equal level both "conjugal love" and "the responsible transmission of life."[3] Thus official Catholic thought recognizes sexuality not only in respect of procreation, but also in terms of the mutuality and the goodness of sexual love. This is what we need to turn our attention to now.

Catechism of the Catholic Church and the Sacrament of Matrimony

There is no better place to find a synthesis of the church's teaching on marriage than the *Catechism of the Catholic Church*.[4] It draws upon Holy Scripture and the church's tradition, most noticeably the theology of marriage in Vatican II's document *Gaudium et Spes*. Scripture begins with marriage, the creation of man and woman in the image and likeness of God in Genesis 1:26–27, and ends with marriage, the nuptials of the Lamb in Revelation 19:7, 9. God himself is described as "the author of marriage" (§1603). Thus the love of man and woman becomes an image of "the absolute and unfailing love with which God loves man" (§1604).

On a practical level, the *Catechism* is all too aware of those features of human sinfulness that can threaten the reality of marriage: "discord, a spirit of domination, infidelity, jealousy, and conflicts that can escalate into hatred and separation" (§1606). This brings into play the importance of dying to self and selfishness. The paschal character of Christian marriage is underscored: "It is by following Christ, renouncing themselves, and taking up their crosses that spouses will be able to 'receive' the original meaning of marriage and live it with the help of Christ. This grace of Christian marriage is a fruit of Christ's cross, the source of all Christian life" (§1615).

The *Catechism* highlights the central passage of Ephesians 5:25–26 on marriage as a mystery participating in and revealing something of the union of Christ and his Church (§1616–1617). It also sees the covenant of marriage integrated into God's covenant with man, so that "Authentic married love is caught up into divine love" (§1639).

It is only after having spoken of this great theological vision of marriage that the *Catechism* goes on to comment on procreation, children, and the openness to fertility (§1652–1654). This makes of marriage and the family the "domestic church," in which persons are formed and shaped to be disciples of Christ (§1655–1656). This is the central teaching about Christian marriage in our tradition, immediately recognizable to any deacon. However, most deacons are married. So it might be interesting to see a married bishop thematize this same teaching some centuries before Vatican II.

Bishop Jeremy Taylor and the Theology of Marriage

Jeremy Taylor (1613–1667) was an Anglican bishop and theologian, one of the greatest preachers of his day. It may seem odd in a book on the theology of the permanent diaconate to turn to an Anglican bishop for guidance, and furthermore, to one who lived in the seventeenth century. But Jeremy Taylor was a bishop who was married and who also wrote finely about marriage. Moreover, Taylor's theology in some important respects anticipates the marital perspective of Vatican II's *Gaudium et Spes* and the *Catechism of the Catholic Church*. He preached two sermons on *The Marriage Ring*, which were published in 1653, the year his first wife died. At the time, various theories of marriage were being discussed in England, ranging from the traditional sacramental view of marriage to marriage understood as an ordinance of the state. Taylor advocates the traditional view, but because of his own lived experience his understanding of it is marked throughout by a certain persuasiveness.

One of these sermons takes as its text the passage in Ephesians 5:32–33: "This is a great mystery, and I am applying it to Christ and the church. Each of you, however, should love his wife as himself, and a wife should respect her husband."[5] Taylor's exegesis finds an echo in the *Catechism*. The sermon offers a profound theology of marriage, and yet, undoubtedly arising out of his own experience, it also grasps the importance of ordinary duties. One author puts it like this: "He moves from the generality of mystery to the particularity of duty."[6] "The first blessing God gave to man was society," writes Taylor, "and that society was a marriage, and that marriage was confederate by God himself, and hallowed by a blessing."[7] Marriage is no afterthought on God's part, but "the first blessing" given to humankind. The word "confederate" is strange to us, but it derives from the Latin for "covenant," *foedus*. Taylor means us to understand that God co-covenants with the covenanted marriage partners, that he is involved and present in their marriage relationship. God's "confederacy" in marriage is Taylor's way of insisting on what today would be referred to as sacramental participation in God.[8] Put this alongside *Gaudium et Spes* and one recognizes an almost identical theology: "For God himself is the author of matrimony, endowed as it is with various benefits and purposes."[9] God's confederacy in marriage is paralleled in the *Catechism* (§1639), citing this passage from *Gaudium et Spes*.

When Taylor says that marriage is "the seminary of the church, and daily brings forth sons and daughters unto God," he is playing on the Latin root, *semen*, "seed." Marriage is the seedbed of the church, the creative ground of her sons and daughters. This is the *Catechism*'s "domestic church" in all but name. He is careful to point up the equal worth of marriage and celibacy in the sight of God, and yet he is very conscious of the ecclesial dimension of marriage:

> The state of marriage fills up the numbers of the elect, and hath in the labour of love, and the delicacies of friendship, the blessing of society, and the union of hands and hearts...it is more merry and more sad [than the single life]; is fuller of sorrows, and fuller of joys; it lies under more burdens, but is supported by all the strengths of love and charity; and those burdens are delightful. Marriage is the mother of the world, and preserves kingdoms, and fills cities, and churches, and heaven itself.[10]

There is much in this magnificent passage. At the biographical level, one can hear Taylor's pain as he recalls the death of his wife and of his children—marriage is "more sad, fuller of sorrows." Yet, at the same time, it is marked by the "delicacies of friendship," is "fuller of joys," and its burdens are "delightful." Without the bond of marriage, there are no people: it is the "mother of the world." It also fills heaven.

While the single life may make people angelic, marriage makes "the chaste pair to be like Christ."[11] Marriage sacramentally represents the union of Christ with the church. Taylor has a mystical view of marriage and its sacramentality: "'This is a great mystery,' but it is the symbolical and sacramental representation of the greatest mysteries of our religion. Christ descended from his Father's bosom, and contracted his divinity with flesh and blood, and married our nature, and we became a Church, the spouse of the Bridegroom...."[12] Marriage is no mere external imitation of Christ's union with the church, but rather it is a sacramental participation in that union.[13] Again, an almost identical passage from *Gaudium et Spes* springs to mind: "The Savior of men and the Spouse of the Church comes into the lives of married Christians through the sacrament of matrimony....Authentic married love is caught up into divine love...."[14] Again, this passage finds its way into the *Catechism,* as we have seen above.

Taylor is practical in his understanding of the sacrament. "Man and wife are equally concerned to avoid all offences of each other in the beginning of their conversation; every little thing can blast an infant blossom...."[15] The couple avoid offense and nurture one another like a delicate blossom. "Let the husband and wife infinitely avoid a curious distinction of mine and thine, for this hath caused all the laws and all the suits and all the wars in the world; let them who have but one person have also but one interest."[16] A man of his own time, as is each of us, Taylor entertains notions coming from his culture about the obedience and inferiority of a wife to her husband. Nevertheless he is equally emphatic that "A husband's power over his wife is paternal and friendly, not magisterial and despotic."[17] And he further remarks: "Above all the instances of love let him preserve toward her an inviolable faith, and an unspotted chastity; for this is the marriage-ring; it ties two hearts by an eternal band....Nothing but death can do so much evil to the holy rites of marriage, as unchastity and breach of faith can...."[18]

Though from within the frame of Taylor's time and culture, the sermon gives us a theology of marriage, understood as self-gift, self-donation, diaconal, and sacramental. The high sacramental vision is matched by its definitive performance indicators.

The Rites of Marriage and Ordination

In the Catholic tradition the sacraments of Marriage and Orders endure for the entire lives of the married and the ordained, until death, with both marriage and ordination to the diaconate understood as self-gift and self-giving. The sacraments begin with the public celebration of the rites, but do not end there. The Rite of Marriage begins with the priest or deacon addressing the couple to be married with these or similar words: "My dear friends, you have come together in this church in the presence of the Church's minister and this community. Christ abundantly blesses this love. He has already consecrated you in baptism and now he enriches you by a special sacrament so that you may assume the duties of marriage in mutual and lasting fidelity...."[19] In this address baptism is recognized as the basic sacrament out of which marriage has grown.

Marriage is described as a sacrament of enrichment and strengthening. The duties of marriage are to be assumed in mutual and lasting fidelity. The minister then proceeds to ask the couple: "Have you come here freely and without reservation to give yourselves to each other in marriage? Will you love and honor each other as husband and wife for the rest of your lives?" Marriage, again, is self-gift, one to the other, "for the rest of your lives." There is a fine sentence in Pope Paul VI's *Humanae Vitae* underscoring this mutual gift of self: "Whoever truly loves his marriage partner loves not only for what he receives, but for the partner's self, rejoicing that he can enrich his partner with the gift of himself."[20] Faithfulness and permanence are emphasized. The faithful self-gift, one to the other, is then pledged in the declaration of consent by the bride and the groom, and is given expression in the exchange of rings in the name of the Trinity. The *Ratio* provides a summary of this view of marriage for a deacon: "For married candidates, to live love means offering themselves to their spouses in a reciprocal belonging, in a total, faithful and indissoluble union, in the likeness of Christ's love for his Church."[21]

The diaconate, too, begins with a public celebration of rites. It "is conferred through a special outpouring of the Spirit [ordination], which brings about in the one who receives it a specific conformation to Christ, Lord and servant of all."[22] The Rite of Ordination of a Deacon commences with the calling and presentation of the candidate, the election by the bishop, and the consent of the assembly. After the homily, there takes place the examination of the candidate, in which the bishop asks five questions about his willingness to serve the people of God, according to the mind of the church. The promise of obedience to the bishop is followed by the

Litany of Saints, the laying on of hands, and the prayer of consecration. This beautiful prayer contains the following words:

> Almighty God...You make the Church, Christ's Body, grow to its full stature as a new and greater temple. You enrich it with every kind of grace and perfect it with a diversity of members to serve the whole body in a wonderful pattern of unity. You established a threefold ministry of worship and service for the glory of your name....Lord, send forth upon him the Holy Spirit, that he may be strengthened by the gift of your sevenfold grace to carry out faithfully the work of the ministry....May he in this life imitate your Son, who came not to be served but to serve, and one day reign with him in heaven....

The prayer describes ordination as an enrichment and strengthening to serve the local church faithfully in self-gift. Finally, the deacon is invested with the stole and dalmatic, and presented with the book of the gospels.

A careful reading of both the Rite of Marriage and the Rite of Ordination indicates very close similarities between them. Both marriage and ordination are sacraments of enrichment and strengthening; both are sacraments of self-donation, to one's spouse, and to the local church through the bishop; both sacraments are permanent; both have external signs of fidelity and of the pledge made.

The Equality of the Sacraments of Marriage and Ordination

No one would question for a moment that the Sacrament of Orders invites and enables the ordinand to encounter and engagement of God-in-Christ. Sometimes, however, there is a sense that the Sacrament of Marriage is not quite equal in this regard. Central to the Sacrament of Marriage is the right ordering of sexuality, one of the most powerful of human forces and dynamics. Yet there is a certain general reluctance to acknowledge the experience of sexuality as God-given and as a mediating encounter with God. Probing the reasons for this reluctance would demand a multi-disciplinary, co-operative effort, but some words of Karl Rahner, S.J., might alert us to the central importance of the issue:

> It must always be borne in mind...that in a true theology of marriage, marriage must really and truly not be regarded as a mere concession to human weakness (a conception attempted over and over again by an almost Manichean intellectual undercurrent in the Church), but must be seen to have an absolutely positive and essential function, not only in the private Christian life of certain individuals, but also in the Church. Marriage, understood as a sacramentally consecrated union, is both in and for the Church the concrete and real representation and living example of the mystery of Christ's union with the Church.[23]

Our experience tells us that Rahner, retrieving the church's traditional affirmations of marriage and marital sexuality here, is absolutely right. The bliss of falling in love with someone, the experience of love-making, the intensity of our attraction to another person—the cumulative, *positive* impact of these experiences suggests powerfully that human sexuality is indeed of God and is not without the presence of God.

A powerful narrative statement of the human-Christian reluctance to grasp the spirituality and sacredness of sexuality is available in Alan Paton's novel *Too Late the Phalarope*.[24] In this story one of the central characters, Pieter van Vlaanderen, a devout South African Christian and a policeman, has a very difficult and taxing relationship with his wife, Nella. Nella has had a strict, Calvinist upbringing, as a result of which she cannot believe that human sexual pleasure is a good thing. In the course of the novel, Pieter speaks as follows: "And I wanted to cry out at her that I could not put the body apart from the soul, and that the comfort of her body was more than a thing of the flesh, but was also a thing of the soul, and why it was, I could not say, and why it should be, I could not say, but there was in it nothing that was ugly or evil, but only good. But how can one find such words?"[25]

Sexuality is not of the soul that Nella equates with goodness and, therefore, sexuality cannot be of God. She subscribes to the latent Manicheanism of which Rahner speaks, and not to the Hebrew and Christian doctrine of creation, with its basis in the creation narratives of the Book of Genesis.

In the account of Genesis 1:1—2.4a, the nucleus of the meaning of creation is found in the refrain, "And God saw that it was good," the refrain being repeated in 1:10, 12, 18, 21, 25. After the creation of male and female in the image of God (vv. 26–27), that is, after the creation of sexuality, comes the affirmation of v. 31: "God saw everything he had made, and indeed, it was *very good*" (my emphasis). Sexuality in the creation account is God's very good gift.[26] The Presbyterian theologian, Robert McAfee Brown, describes the human person like this: "...a total being who can do many different things—think, fight, remember, love, anticipate, copulate, sing, laugh, imagine. *All* the activities can be used for good ends, all can be abused and turned to evil ends."[27] Human sexuality and spirituality are not opposites, but are intimately and inseparably bound together.

A clear and tragic example of the negative consequences of failing to recognize this offers itself in the person of the great Danish philosopher Søren Kierkegaard (1813–1855).[28] In 1841 he became engaged to Regina Olsen. Fearing that marriage to Regina might distract him from a total commitment to and love of God, he broke off the engagement. The Jewish philosopher Martin Buber comments on Kierkegaard's decision:

> That is sublimely to misunderstand God. Creation is not a hurdle on the road to God, it is the road itself. We are created along with one another and directed to a life with one another. Creatures are placed in my way so that I, their fellow-creature, by means of them and with them, find the way to God. A God reached by their exclusion would not be the God of all lives in whom all life is fulfilled...God wants us to come to [God] by means of the Reginas [God] has created, and not by renunciation of them.[29]

Failing and Falling

The vision of marriage set out in Jeremy Taylor, in Vatican II, and in the Rite of Marriage is an ideal after which the diaconal couple must strive. However, honesty demands of a deacon, as indeed it does of everyone, that he recognize the deficits in his marriage; integrity demands that he do something about them. Just as a daily examination of conscience will throw up all too quickly the deficits in our diaconal service, so the examination will also point out the *lacunae* in our marital service. In his poem "Discipline," the priest-poet George Herbert (1593–1633), the friend of Deacon Nicholas Ferrar, writes:

> Though I fail, I weep:
> Though I halt in pace,
> Yet I creep to the throne of grace.[30]

All serious Christians, and here especially deacons, know in their hearts their failures and their "haltings in pace" when it comes to marriage. The striving after the ideal, marked by consistent and daily conversion, is everything. "Psychologists tell us that a true friend is someone who has seen us at our worst and still loves us."[31] The ongoing acknowledgment of fault and deficit, the confession of the absence of the marital virtues described by Jeremy Taylor, and the constant striving to serve better make up the profile of serious Christian marriages. Sometimes, however, problems are deeper— and grow deeper still—and marriage ends in divorce.

Divorce is a most complicated matter, but it is, at least, a public and legal statement that a marriage has broken down irretrievably. The church finds the situation of the divorced deacon very difficult because of the clear ecclesial teaching on the indissolubility of marriage, and also because of the public ecclesial role of the deacon. How is one to comment on this sensitive issue in respect of deacons without useless generalizing?

The recent work of the accomplished Christian novelist Susan Howatch is helpful here—helpful in that it glosses marital failure in a clerical context—and not because it solves problems. In her novel *Absolute Truths,* the Anglican Bishop of Starbridge, Dr. Charles Ashworth, is faced with the request to receive divorced priest Lewis Hall into his diocese. Ashworth is of two minds about it as he contemplates all the possible problems: for example, the possibility of scandal, the issue of re-marriage, the awkward social situation of such a clergyman at diocesan events, the theological anomaly. As it happens, however, Lewis Hall becomes an instrument of God's grace not only to the run-down parish in which he serves, but also to the spiritual life of Bishop Ashworth himself. Ashworth finds in this maritally broken clergyman a sure spiritual guide. One thinks immediately of the Pauline theme of strength being made perfect in weakness (1 Cor 1:20–31). Today's divorced deacon, due to his very public position in the church, points to the complex tragedy of broken marriage. But, as with Lewis Hall, the divorced deacon may become a tangible living sign of *hope*. Our flawed human nature, the consequence and expression of original sin, which infects our lives and relationships, does not have the last word. With God's grace and ongoing spiritual direction and discernment, the divorced deacon may have an enduring role and witness and contribution in the church. His self-donation to the wider community of the church remains even as his service to his spouse fragments. Though he fails, the divorced deacon weeps; though he halts in pace, he creeps to the throne of grace.

Conclusion

Ultimately, and at its best, our sexual-marital experience in a special way intimates to us that God wants us—that God passionately wants us! The whole point of creation, redemption, and consummation is to underscore God's passion for us. Here is how Archbishop Rowan Williams of Canterbury puts it: "The whole story of creation, incarnation and our incorporation into the fellowship of Christ's body tells us that God desires us, *as if we were God,* as if we were that unconditional response to God's giving that God's self makes in the life of the Trinity. We are created so that we may be caught up in this, so that we may grow into the wholehearted love of God by learning that God loves us as God loves God." [32] Much of the time we love and experience love as who we are, freighted down with baggage and preconditions and presuppositions. Marriage as a sacrament catches us up in the wholehearted love of God, and invites us to the performance of that love by a constant dying to egocentricity and a rising to centeredness in God. Deacons and deacon couples are a particularly public demonstration to live and love as God.

The Dysfunctional Deacon

*Anything deacons do to stir up the people, nurture their
activity, and get them up and moving turns a corpse into
a lively body.*[1]

This book about the diaconate has been trying to shape a
vision and understanding of the diaconate that will contribute to
stirring up the people and helping them to experience themselves
more deeply as the Body of Christ. It is, however, one thing to shape
a vision and understanding, and something else to perform and to
enact it. It is here that failure occurs, and it is to an examination of
the diaconal conscience that we now turn.

The cliché "No one is perfect" is a cliché because it is true: we
all make mistakes and cultivate habits that impede our being drawn
into intimacy with God. We fail and halt in pace, but we keep going.
If we are to gain real self-knowledge as deacons, it is essential that
we examine corporately and individually our consciences and that
we have regard to diaconal dysfunctions. There are dysfunctional
diaconal traits that concern the deacon and the church, and dysfunctional diaconal traits that concern the deacon and his family. In
respect of the deacon and the church one may point to such traits
that impede *diakonia: ritualism, clericalism, anti-intellectualism,
crusadism* and *negativism.* Add to this list those characteristics that
may obtain in a deacon's relationship with his family: *messianism*
and *exemplarism.*

Ritualism

Ritualism is the tendency of deacons to get "hung up" on liturgical rites rather than attending to authentic liturgical service. A
proper attendance to liturgical rites is not ritualism. Knowing the

rites in detail and using them in personal prayer and spirituality in such a way that the liturgy flows smoothly and with dignity enhances diaconal participation and serves the assembly. However, this does not always occur. Bishop John F. Kinney, addressing the National Catholic Diaconate Conference in New Orleans in 1994, had some critical remarks to make about the liturgical ministry of deacons: "Deacons need to be excellent in the liturgy, not second-rate as some of them are perceived to be. It takes study and practice and preparation. I know of no other way to be a good liturgist than study, practice and preparation."[2] The deacon must strive for excellence in the liturgy because, in the expression of Aidan Kavanagh, O.S.B., "he is the assembly's prime minister."[3] The deacon's role as "butler in God's house, *major domo* of its banquet, master of its ceremonies" demands the excellent liturgical performance that enables prayerful participation by the entire assembly, including the other ministers.[4] This is not ritualism, but service, *diakonia*.

A symptom of ritualism is when a deacon gets upset when someone else usurps his place in the liturgy, by word or action, intentionally or unintentionally. Confusion about or ignorance of the proper liturgical role of the deacon is quite widespread and should be corrected by more adequate liturgical education. But the identity of a deacon should not be so tied to the *minutiae* of the liturgy that he feels diminished when this confusion or ignorance occurs. In fact it is in these moments of public confusion at liturgy that a deacon can show his love of neighbor by perseverance and courteous behavior.

Clericalism

Clericalism is an excessive consciousness of being a deacon, a sense of superiority flowing from membership in the clerical "club," and a failure to appreciate the sacrament of baptism shared by other Christians. Bishop Dale Melczek goes on to specify clericalism as "an ordained ministry that has grown fat, self-serving and self-sufficient."[5]

It is true that a deacon is a cleric, a member of the clergy; he is not a lay minister, a "lay deacon," which is a common assumption on the part of the laity. A deacon's awareness of his ordained status is not clericalism. Clericalism happens when a deacon feels unappreciated, unaccepted, unaffirmed, especially by others in Orders, and then compensates for the relationship deficit by over-emphasizing his clerical status. It is both artificially contrived and very destructive, particularly for the deacon himself. Contrast that kind of clericalism with the most prominent cleric in the world, Pope John Paul II. The Holy Father is fond of citing St. Augustine's often-repeated phrase, "For you I am a bishop, with you I am a Christian." John Paul II adds: "On further reflection, *Christian* has far greater significance than *bishop,* even if the subject is the Bishop of Rome."[6] Here is a true appreciation of what it is to be a member of the clergy and a true appreciation of holy baptism. Clergy are first Christians with other Christians; their office is to serve and sustain the Christian body corporate of which, through baptism, they are privileged to be members.

Anti-Intellectualism

"Candidates should be predisposed to continuing their formation after ordination. To this end, they are encouraged to establish a small personal library with a theological-pastoral emphasis and to be open to programs of ongoing formation."[7] These words of the *Ratio* need to be taken seriously. Sometimes one hears clergy, both deacons and priests, favoring the "pastoral" over the "theological." The pastoral work and the pastoral demands of the church figure largely in their perceptions and ought to do so, but not when theology is seen as marginal to that work. How could a surgeon find research in his field marginal to what he does? It is no different for one in Orders. "There is a widespread attitude in society that elevates activity at the expense of thought and disciplined study, which devalues pure research in favour of applied, which turns the word 'academic' into a word of criticism, a synonym for 'irrelevant,' 'impractical' or 'niggling'....And this mood has invaded the Church."[8] This is anti-intellectualism, and it is sheerly incredible—not to say distressing—for at least two reasons.

First, it shows a most naive attitude toward both pastoral work and prayer and spirituality. When an ordained person is working in the area of marriage, he is necessarily working with some understanding of what marriage is. That understanding involves theology, as well as other fields, especially the human sciences. The presuppositions that he brings to his pastoral work are theological. Or, if a deacon is working in the area of baptism preparation, whether for an infant or in the Order for the Christian Initiation of Adults, an entire host of theological presuppositions comes into play: What is a sacrament? What is the relationship between nature and grace? What is grace? How does grace work, or does it, for those who have no exposure to the church or the sacraments? It is simply impossible to get away from theology in either pastoral ministry or in one's own prayer life.

The question is not whether to interest oneself in theology or pastoral ministry. Rather, the question is "Is my pastoral work informed by solid and continuing work in theology? Or is my pastoral work stagnant because I have ceased to study?" Aidan Nichols, O.P., gives particular emphasis to the necessity of ongoing study for one who claims to have even basic and rudimentary competence in theology: "To be a theological student in the full sense of those words cannot be a temporary state or a preamble to something else, such as the ministerial priesthood [or the diaconate] or an all-round education. Rather, it is a solemn engagement to developing over the course of a lifetime the gift of Christian wonder or curiosity....As theologians, then, we commit ourselves to the lifelong study and reflection which the satisfaction of such curiosity will need."[9]

There is a second reason why anti-intellectualism is incredible: it is a betrayal of the trust of the people of God. Theology is a solemn engagement to developing, *over a lifetime,* the gift of Christian wonder or curiosity. That is what people expect of us. People do not expect the deacon to study and absorb detailed presentations that come out regularly on every aspect of theology. But if a deacon does not strive to study regularly and constantly, in accord with his holy office in the church, the church suffers and so does he. The people have a right to expect that the deacon will preach and teach adequately, in accordance with his ordination mandate. That demands much study. As Frances M. Young puts it, "If the Christian community is to witness to the reality of God's presence in the world, it needs ministers and clergy who accept the daunting but exciting task of theological enquiry."[10]

Crusadism

As with these other traits, crusadism is far from being exclusive to deacons. It occurs when a deacon becomes a "one issue minister," overenthusiastic about a particular issue until it becomes almost his exclusive concern. It is his personal crusade, as it were. At every opportunity this one issue gets aired, preached, and acted upon, as though nothing else counted or mattered in the church. What issues do I have in mind? One could find many examples, ranging from pro-life issues, to eucharistic adoration, to Marian devotions, to social justice issues. Such issues are necessary and important, and they belong to the rich patrimony and tradition of the church. Dysfunctionality occurs when an issue gets singled out and becomes identified with the deacon.

Negativism

The fifth dysfunctional characteristic is negativism. It is found in many and varied sectors of society. Nevertheless, it is possible to point to what one might call a general clerical malaise, which finds constant expression in carping criticism and fault-finding with all manner of things in the church. Either the church is too conservative or it is too reactionary, or the shortage of priests bodes the end of the church as we know it, and so on and so forth. This kind of negativism is infectious, betraying a lack of faith in the Holy Spirit's guidance. The most effective antidote to negativism is a sound spiritual life that includes a healthy pride in the church, a pride that does not prevent the recognition of human sinfulness, but also sees the manifestations of divine glory in the church; a pride that enables one to give the church one's wholehearted, but critical, loyalty. Attention will be devoted to this issue in a more positive vein in the chapter "Loving the Church."

Messianism

The Messiah is God's agent for the radical renewal and total transformation of the world, the one who will bring God's purposes for the world to fulfillment. *Messianism* is when the deacon believes, "Without *me,* the church will fall apart." The messianic deacon wants to be involved in everything. At one level this expresses great and highly commendable enthusiasm. At the level of realism, however, messianism is a recipe for abject disaster. No deacon is competent to do everything in a parish. And no deacon should feel that he needs to compensate for what is not being done by others. The entire parish should exemplify a network of collaborative ministries, in which the deacon has a place of servant leadership. He should not feel responsible for everything, nor should he feel guilty about feeling that he is not responsible for everything. Messianism translates into the attitude, "If I don't do it all by myself, nothing will get done." There is no need to comment on how such an attitude will impact the deacon's wife and family.

Exemplarism

Exemplarism comes from the Latin word *exemplum,* meaning "example." Good example is a moral obligation for all Christians, flowing from their baptism into Christ. Every Christian has a responsibility to build up the body of Christ, not least by the personal example he or she gives. That is not what is intended by *exemplarism.* Exemplarism occurs when a deacon feels that his wife and family need to be flagships of familial propriety and domestic perfection: no harsh words, no relational difficulties, attendance at every parish and diocesan function, no doubts or difficulties with the faith. Exemplarism is grossly unfair to both the deacon's family and to himself because it imposes unrealistic expectations, and the failure to realize them becomes a major source of stress, personal and familial. The varieties of temperament, character, and stages of intellectual, moral, and emotional development and maturity, which are featured in every family, are also present in a diaconal family. The *deacon* was ordained, *not* his family. While support from them is a normal and just expectation, neither he nor they should have ideals expected of them nor demands made of them which, in principle, would not be expected or made of any other family in the parish community.

Once again fiction can be of assistance to us in our reflections, this time in a novel of Joanna Trollope, *The Rector's Wife.*[11] At one level Trollope's novel is a story about the attractions of adultery when a marriage has reached a dead end. At a deeper level, however, the novel is about what happens to individuals and their relationships when public expectations conflict with the realities and demands of their private lives. The rector in *The Rector's Wife,* Peter Bouverie, has spent his life and defined his ministry according to what other people think, and he expects his family to do the same. The resulting tension is evident throughout the entire book. Gossiping village women become silent, or better fall silent, when Anna Bouverie, Peter's wife, joins them. Their daughter is most unhappy at school, because she is singled out as the rector's daughter and is the butt of taunts and jibes. Peter does not permit his wife to teach—she is a linguist—because some of his parishioners might object to the rector's wife working. So Anna spends her time working on small translation jobs, worrying about the family's dismal financial state, and performing the many parish tasks that are taken for granted both by her husband and his parishioners.

Eventually, after Peter is passed over for a promotion to which he thought he was entitled, his ministry and his marriage dry up. Anna seeks liberation in various ways, but her liberation is seen by Peter only as a series of betrayals. She has reneged on her proper role as the rector's wife. The real root issue of Trollope's novel is that Peter and Anna Bouverie's sense of identity both as individuals and as a couple is constantly being defined by the expectations of other people. Peter Bouverie has internalized what I have described as *exemplarism,* and this drives his self-understanding, his ministry, and his marriage.

Although the Bouverie' story is an extreme case, their predicament is one that deacon couples can understand. "Our special need is not to see ourselves as others see us, but to retain the integrity of that part of our lives that others do not see."[12]

10

Loving the Church

We need a Catholic revival....The story of God's love must be told in (at least) a thousand different ways and lived by those who tell it (as best they can). I do not blame priests and deacons and their preaching for the malaise. However, as teachers and leaders, who else but priests and deacons will lead the revival that we so desperately need?[1]

There is no need to commend a love of the church to deacons. Their service to the church is the expression of that love. Sometimes, however, it just feels good and right to say it. I am thinking, for example, of that fine little book by the French Dominican Cardinal Yves Congar (1904–1995), with the title *This Church That I Love.*[2] In the "Foreword" Congar writes about the three intertwined loves of his life: church, laity, and priesthood. Could not we as deacons alter those loves for ourselves: church, laity, and diaconate? Without that basic love for the church, we would not continue to serve.

Scandal in the Church

Today it is impossible to speak credibly of love for the church without confronting the question of grave scandal. Many Catholics are properly outraged by priests who committed sexual misconduct with minors, and even more by bishops who continued to reassign such offenders, providing them with even further opportunity to offend. How are we to address this grave and complex issue? First, by recognizing that there always have been scandals in the church and there will continue to be. This is not to minimize in any degree the harm done, nor the scandal given. It is simply to acknowledge the reality of sin. We cannot, however, remain stuck in that acknowledgment, for that would concede everything to the powers of evil. We need also to recognize the holiness that is all too often hidden in the ordinary members of the church as they strive to remain faithful. John C. Cavadini describes it as spouses "heroically faithful to each other and to the care of their children, yet it yields only what looks to be a 'normal' life." In the face of such extraordinary but ordinary hidden holiness we need to respond to the challenge to go beyond the horror and the scandal. He also writes: "In reacting to a scandal it is wise to remember that our own proclivity to overlook and downplay the goodness which would challenge us is itself a liability. For it is only by looking at that goodness, by acquiring the habit of noticing it, that we will find the inspiration and the courage to re-imagine a future for the church beyond the impasse that seems thrust upon us."[3] Careful attention to the good and the holiness that is all around us will bring a degree of perspective in the face of scandal, but much more will it alert us to the fact that grace abounds in all kinds of wonderful ways. Despite the besmirching of scandal, in Gerard Manley Hopkins's words,

> The world is charged with the grandeur of God.
> It will flame out, like shining from shook foil.[4]

For one who loves the church, scandal is an invitation to deeper personal holiness and to developing eyes of faith that see beyond, all the while confessing and reforming, the immediacy of sin.

Is it out of place to suggest that, as part of this love, there is a proper kind of pride in the church? Pride, of course, conjures up the deadly vices to which human life is prone: pride, envy, anger, sloth, avarice, gluttony, and lust. Indeed pride has been regarded as the most primordial of sins from which the others are derived. Think of the comment of St. Augustine, who traces back even sins of the flesh to pride: "If anyone says that the flesh is the cause of all the vices and ill conduct, it is certain that he has not carefully considered the whole nature of man....Of all these evils, pride is the origin, and it rules in the devil, though he has no flesh."[5]

Undoubtedly there is a wrong kind of pride in the church. This finds expression in a variety of ways, for example, the feeling of self-righteousness among members of the church, which offers the attractive illusion of feeling holier and better than others, and among those Christians who are no longer formally active as church. There is also the proud attitude of superiority toward members of other faiths, displaying too often an ignorance of our own faith as much as the faith of others. Closely allied to this is the arrogant assumption that Christians have a monopoly on "the truth, the whole truth, and nothing but the truth." Finally, one might point to that kind of false ecclesial pride that finds expression in "an eagerness for preferment scarcely appropriate in those who counted themselves ministers or servants of Jesus Christ."[6]

If we leave to one side these false forms of pride in the church, in addressing a right pride we could not do better than take our cue from the nature of the One whom we profess to follow. As Christ was sent by the Father, so the church is sent by the Holy Spirit in Christ. There is no Christ without the church, no church without Christ. As John Macquarrie puts it, "The church is not the Kingdom of God, but it is the people of God, a part of humanity where God is seeking to manifest his purpose for the whole human race."[7] If we take our cue even further from Christology, from the Council of Chalcedon (451), then we might come up with something like this: "Christ is as divine as the Father and as human as we are, sin excepted; the church, that is ourselves, is made divine in Christ, sin accepted."

In developing our love for the church and a right pride in the church, we need to lay alongside those glorious images of the church as Body of Christ, Herald of the Kingdom, and Sacrament of the Divine Communion, the insight of St. Augustine that the church is a hospital for incurables, a hospital for sinners. The church is holy through the graceful initiative of God, but it is made up of sinners. There is no avoidance of sinners in God's divine activity in the church. As Yves Congar comments: "[All the manifold functions of the church] are performed by men in the course of history in which neither grace nor the real and creative visitations of the Holy Spirit permit to stride miraculously over the boundaries, to avoid detours, blind alleys, delays, and even errors."[8] The Holy Spirit works through the sinners that we are, never without us.

A rightful pride in the church points to two things. First, the liturgy of the church. When conducted with due dignity, according to the mind of the church in her documentation and guidelines, the liturgy not only offers praise to God, but is something of which we may rightly be proud.[9] The music, the decorum of the ministers, the care with which the Scriptures are announced and the homily proclaimed, the beauty of the building—of all of these we may rightly be proud. Deacons are intimately linked with the careful choreography of the liturgy according to *Lumen Gentium* §29: "It is the duty of the deacon, to the extent that he has been authorized by competent authority, to administer baptism solemnly, to be custodian and dispenser of the Eucharist, to assist at and bless marriages in the name of the Church, to bring Viaticum to the dying, to read the sacred Scripture to the faithful...to preside at the worship and prayer of the faithful...."[10] A proper pride in the liturgy should accompany a deacon.

Second, we may be rightly proud of the church's commitment to social justice. The twentieth century has witnessed the church proclaiming social justice clearly in a series of papal encyclicals. From Pope Leo XIII's *Rerum Novarum* of 1891 to Pope John Paul II's *Centesimus Annus* of 1991, the magisterium has consistently proclaimed that issues of social justice pertain to the church's evangelizing mission and are "an essential part of the Christian message."[11] There has been no complete and unequivocal condemnation of socialism nor endorsement of capitalism on the part of the church in these encyclical letters so much as the constant affirmation that all political economies must have the well-being of persons at their center, in such a fashion that persons can never be a means to an end. A concern for justice is also part of the deacon profile, according to *Lumen Gentium* §29: "Dedicated to duties of charity and of administration, let deacons be mindful of the admonition of Blessed Polycarp: 'Be merciful, diligent, walking according to the truth of the Lord, who became the servant of all.'"[12] Implied in this statement is the conviction that justice is the working out of charity, and appropriate administration the prerequisite for justice. And this is explicitly described as the work of deacons. The church's record on justice is one of which we may rightly be proud.

In a book published shortly before his death, the great French theologian Cardinal Jean Daniélou, S.J. (1905–1974), wrote: "Many Christians today give the impression that they do not feel at ease in the church, and that they only remain faithful to her with difficulty. I must say that my experience is contrary. The church has never disappointed me. It is rather I who would be inclined to accuse myself of not having drawn profit enough from all she has to offer me."[13] I wish I could say that without qualification. Sometimes I do feel disappointed with the church, not least with the pettiness of myself and other Catholics, including fellow deacons. Such disappointment can never be a final resting point without reducing our lives and our faith to absurdity. Thinking about our families may help here. There are times when, as parents, we experience disappointment with our children, especially when they are moving through those tempestuous years into early adulthood. But we do not cease to love them. When we feel disappointment with the church, especially as deacons, let us see if we have drawn enough profit from all she has to offer us and let us seek solutions to our disappointment, but never cease to love this church in whom, in Christ, we live and move and have our being. Let us pledge to be part of the revival called for by Fr. Andrew Greeley at the outset of this chapter, and which we know in our hearts to be so sorely needed in this church that we love: "We need a Catholic revival....The story of God's love must be told."

Notes

Introduction

1. Congregation for Catholic Education, *Basic Norms for the Formation of Permanent Deacons,* Vatican City: Libreria Editrice Vaticana, 1998, #3. This title is hereafter abbreviated as *Ratio.*

Chapter 1

1. Introduction to the *Ratio.* Also, the Congregation for the Clergy, *Directory for the Ministry and Life of Permanent Deacons,* Vatican City: Libreria Editrice Vaticana, 1998, #2. This title is hereafter abbreviated as *Directory.*

2. Avery Dulles, "The Four Faces of American Catholicism," *Louvain Studies* 18 (1993): 99–109.

3. "Evangelical-Catholic" comes from Msgr. Francis Mannion, in a conversation of October 1994. "The new faithful" is, in fact, the title of a very recent book by Colleen Carroll, published by Loyola Press of Chicago, 2002.

4. Dulles, "Four Faces," 103.

5. See Colleen Carroll, *The New Faithful,* Chicago: Loyola Press, 2002, especially 201–5.

6. Ibid., 280.

7. Meriol Trevor, *Prophets and Guardians: Renewal and Tradition in the Church,* Garden City, N.Y.: Doubleday, 1969, 49.

8. Bernard M. G. Reardon, *Roman Catholic Modernism,* Stanford, Calif.: Stanford University Press, 1970, 181.

9. Von Hügel, cited in Reardon, 180.

10. Friedrich von Hugel, *The Mystical Element of Religion,* vol. 1, London: Dent, 1908, xv.

11. Friedrich von Hügel, *Essays and Addresses,* vol. 1, London: Dent, 1921, 293.

12. Ibid., 264.

13. Nicholas Lash, "The Difficulty of Making Sense," *New Blackfriars* 70 (February 1989): 77.

14. Friedrich von Hügel, *Selected Letters,* ed. B. Holland, London: Dent, 1927, 84.

15. Friedrich von Hügel, *Eternal Life,* Edinburgh: T. & T. Clark, 1912, 365.

16. Trevor, *Prophets and Guardians,* 122–23.

17. Ronald Knox, *Enthusiasm,* Oxford: Clarendon Press, 1950.

18. David Tracy, "Freedom, Responsibility, Authority," in *Empowering Authority: The Charisms of Episcopacy and Primacy in the Church Today,* ed. Patrick J. Howell and Gary Chamberlain, Kansas City, Mo.: Sheed and Ward, 1990, 41.

19. Gabriel Daly, O.S.A., *Transcendence and Immanence, A Study in Catholic Modernism and Integralism,* Oxford: Clarendon Press, 1980, 131.

20. Von Hügel, *Mystical Element,* 53.

21. Daly, *Transcendence,* 131.

22. Ibid., 136. This notion is developed in John J. Heaney, *The Modernist Crisis: Von Hügel,* Washington, D.C.: Corpus Books, 1968, 76–82.

23. John Macquarrie, *Thinking About God,* London: SCM Press, 1975, 61. For an introduction to the thought of this outstanding theologian, see Owen F. Cummings, *John Macquarrie, A Master of Theology,* Mahwah, N.J.: Paulist Press, 2002.

24. William T. Donovan, *Sacrament of Service: Understanding Diaconal Spirituality,* Green Bay, Wis.: Alt Publishing Company, 2000, 10.

Chapter 2

1. Paul McPartlan, "The Permanent Diaconate and *Gaudium et Spes,*" *Briefing* 32 (2002): 3. I am much indebted to the outstanding insights of Fr. McPartlan.

2. Avery Dulles, *The Reshaping of Catholicism,* San Francisco: Harper and Row, 1988, 19.

3. Pope John Paul II, *On the Coming of the Third Millennium,* Washington, D.C.: U.S.C.C.B., 1994, par. 36.

4. Pope John Paul II, *Novo Millennio Ineunte,* Washington, D.C.: U.S.C.C.B., 2001, par. 43.

5. *Ratio,* #4.

6. The work of Dennis M. Doyle (*The Church as Communion,* Maryknoll, N.Y.: Orbis Books, 2000) is helpful in distinguishing different but related models of communion ecclesiology.

7. Austin Flannery, O.P., ed., *Vatican Council II, The Conciliar and Postconciliar Documents,* New York: Costello Publishing Company, 1975, 350.

8. Walter Kasper, "The Deacon Offers an Ecclesiological View of the Present Day Challenges in the Church and Society," a paper presented at the International Diaconate Center Study-Conference, Brixen, Italy, October 1997, and available at deacons.net. The citation is from p. 8. All page references are to the 18-page printout from the online reference.

9. McPartlan, *"Gaudium et Spes,"* 3.

10. Enda McDonagh, "The Church in the Modern World," in *Modern Catholicism: Vatican II and After,* ed. Adrian Hastings, New York: Oxford University Press, 1991, 98.

11. McPartlan, *"Gaudium et Spes,"* 4.

12. Ibid.

13. Ibid., 7. Paragraph 22 from *Gaudium et Spes* may be found in Walter M. Abbott, S.J., ed., *The Documents of Vatican II,* New York, 1966, 220.

14. McPartlan, *"Gaudium et Spes,"* 7.

15. Karl Rahner, "The Teaching of the Second Vatican Council on the Diaconate," in *Foundations for the Renewal of the Permanent Diaconate,* Washington, D.C.: United States Conference of Catholic Bishops, 1993, 184.

16. Abbott, *Documents,* 52–53.

17. Kasper, "Ecclesiological View," 4.

18. William Shawn McKnight, *The Latin Rite Deacon: Symbol of Communitas and Social Intermediary Among the People of God,* Rome: Pontificium Athenaeum S. Anselmi, 2001, 342.

19. McPartlan, *"Gaudium et spes,"* 8.

20. Abbott, *Documents,* 55–56.

21. The Irish systematic theologian Seamus Ryan in *The Church, A Theological and Pastoral Commentary on the Constitution on the Church,* ed. Kevin McNamara, Dublin: Veritas Publications, 1983, 231. The original date of this publication was 1968.

22. Ibid., 232.

23. Introduction to the *Ratio,* and *Directory,* #2.

24. Leon J. Suenens, *Coresponsibility in the Church,* New York: Herder and Herder, 1968, 155.

25. Frank C. Senn, "The Ecclesiological Basis of the Office of Deacon," *Pro Ecclesia* 3 (1994): 204.

26. Abbott, *Documents,* 605.

27. McPartlan, *"Gaudium et spes,"* 7.

28. William W. Emilsen, "The Face of Christ: The Ministry of Deacons," *The Expository Times* 110 (April 1999): 217.

Chapter 3

1. Kasper, "Ecclesiological View," 1.

2. James M. Barnett, *The Diaconate, A Full and Equal Order,* rev ed., Valley Forge, Pa.: Trinity Press International, 1995, 19. For the most detailed analysis of the word *diakonia*/service in English, see John N. Collins, *Diakonia, Re-interpreting the Ancient Sources,* New York: Oxford University Press, 1990.

3. Ignatius of Antioch, Letter to the Magnesians, 6.1.

4. Ignatius of Antioch, Letter to the Trallians, 3.1.

5. The hymnic structure here is adapted from Ben Witherington, III, *The Many Faces of the Christ,* New York: Crossroad, 1998, 79. There are many books interpreting and interpreting away this famous Pauline text. I am following Witherington because he seems to stay close to the obvious meaning of the text and, therefore, to the perspective of christological orthodoxy.

6. Ibid., 80.

7. Ibid. A similar point of view is offered by Frank Matera, *New Testament Christology,* Louisville, Ky.: Westminster John Knox Press, 1999, 129–30.

8. Witherington, *Many Faces,* 80.

9. Pheme Perkins, "The Gospel According to John," in *The New Jerome Biblical Commentary,* ed. R. E. Brown, S.S., J. A Fitzmyer, S.J., and R. E. Murphy, O.Carm., Englewood Cliffs, N.J.: Prentice Hall, 1990, 973.

10. Kasper, "Ecclesiological View," 10.

11. William Vanstone, *Love's Endeavour, Love's Expense,* London: Darton, Longman and Todd, 1977, 70.

12. *Ratio, #5,* my emphasis.

13. Kasper, "Ecclesiological View," 6.

14. Ibid., 7, 11. See also the *Ratio, #7.*

15. Donovan, *Sacrament of Service,* 16.

16. Mark Santer, "Diaconate and Discipleship," *Theology* 81 (May 1978): 181–82. This article by Bishop Santer was first preached as a homily at the ordination to the diaconate of Rowan Douglas Williams, now Archbishop of Canterbury.

Chapter 4

1. Karl Rahner, S.J., "On the Diaconate," in *Foundations for the Renewal of the Permanent Diaconate,* Washington, D.C.: United States Conference of Catholic Bishops, 1993, 198.

2. Norbert Brockman, S.M., *Ordained to Serve: A Theology of the Permanent Diaconate,* Smithtown, N.Y.: Exposition Press, 1976, 5. Also, Daniel J. Harrington, S.J. (*The Church According to the New Testament,* Franklin, Wis.: Sheed and Ward, 2001, 160) calls the process of structural development the "routinization of charisma." See also Rahner, "On the Diaconate," 194–95.

3. Edward Echlin, *The Deacon in the Church, Past and Future,* New York: Alba House, 1971, 7.

4. Collins's most comprehensive scholarly publication is his doctoral dissertation at Kings College, University of London, done under the New Testament scholar Christopher Evans, and titled *Diakonia: Re-interpreting the Ancient Sources,* New York: Oxford University Press, 1990. A non-technical but scholarly summary and theological extension of this may be found in his *Are All Christians Ministers?* Newtown, New South Wales: E. J. Dwyer, 1992 (abbreviated here as *All Christians*). Very restricted in scope but very clear in presentation is his article "Learning About Ministry from the

Seven," *Deacon Digest* 15 (May/June, 1998): 26–30 (abbreviated here as "Learning").

5. Collins, *All Christians,* 36.

6. Ibid., 37.

7. Ibid., 39.

8. Collins, "Learning," 28.

9. Lawrence R. Hennessey, S.T., "Diakonia and Diakonos in the Pre-Nicene Church," in *Diakonia: Studies in Honor of Robert T. Meyer,* ed. Thomas Halton and Joseph Williman, Washington, D.C.: The Catholic University of America Press, 1986, 70–71.

10. Irenaeus, *Against the Heresies,* 3.12.10.

11. Hennessey, "Diakonia," 72.

12. Hans Küng, *The Church,* London: Burns and Oates, 1967, 400. See also John N. Collins, *All Christians,* 143. However, Echlin (*Deacon in the Church, 9*), writing of the same passage, does not think that deacons can be clearly differentiated from bishops here, but that seems to me rather stretched.

13. Aimé George Martimort, *Deaconesses: An Historical Study,* trans. K. D. Whitehead, San Francisco: Ignatius Press, 1986, 19–20.

14. Kenan B. Osborne, O.F.M., *The Diaconate in the Christian Church: Its History and Theology,* Chicago: National Association of Diaconate Directors, 1996, 17.

15. Collins, *All Christians,* 71. Collins is drawing upon the work of the New Testament scholar, Robert Jewett, "Paul, Phoebe, and the Spanish Mission," in *The Social World of Formative Christianity and Judaism,* ed. Jacob Neusner and others, Philadelphia: Fortress Press, 1988, 142–61.

16. Echlin, *Deacon,* 10.

17. Osborne, *Diaconate,* 18.

18. Raymond E. Brown, S.S., *Priest and Bishop: Biblical-Reflections,* London: Geoffrey Chapman, 1970, 35.

19. Hennessey, "Diakonia," 73.

20. Jean Paul Audet, *Structures in Christian Priesthood,* New York: Macmillan, 1967, 60.

21. Ibid., 37. I include the deacon as a possible overseer of the communal finances because he is to be "not greedy for sordid gain" (v. 8). This suggests that he had access to moneys other than his own.

22. John Chrysostom, Homily on the Letters to Timothy, 11.

23. John G. Davies, "Deacons, Deaconesses and the Minor Orders in the Patristic Period," *Journal of Ecclesiastical History* 13 (1962): 2.

24. *Didache* 15 in *Early Christian Writings,* rev. ed., edited by Maxwell Staniforth and Andrew Louth, Harmondsworth, U.K.: Penguin Books, 1987, 197.

25. Henry Chadwick, *The Early Church,* rev. ed., Harmondsworth, U.K.: Penguin Books, 1993, 47.

26. Paul Bradshaw, *Liturgical Presidency in the Early Church,* Bramcote, Notts., U.K.: Grove Books, 1983, 9.

27. Echlin, *Deacon,* 17.

28. Hermas, 3 Vis. 5.1.

29. Hermas, *The Shepherd,* Parable 9.26.2.

30. Justin Martyr, *Apology I,* 65.

31. Frank Leslie Cross, *The Early Christian Fathers,* London: Duckworth, 1960, 136.

32. David Rankin, *Tertullian and the Church,* Cambridge: Cambridge University Press, 1995, esp. 143–172.

33. Tertullian, *On Baptism,* 17.

34. Cross, *Early Christian Fathers,* 97.

35. *Didascalia,* chapter 16.

36. Paul McPartlan, "The Permanent Diaconate: Catholic and Ecumenical Perspectives," *Briefing* 32 (2002), 13.

37. Martimort, *Deaconnesses,* 36–37.

38. Ibid.

39. Ibid., 38.

40. Martimort, passim especially 241–50. Cipriano Vagaggini, O.S.B., *L'ordinazione delle diaconesse nella tradizione greca e bizantina,* Rome: O.C.P., 1974, cited in Martimort, 151.

41. Ibid., 245.

42. Hippolytus, *Apostolic Tradition,* 9.

43. Cited from Paul F. Bradshaw, *Ordination Rites of the Ancient Churches of East and West,* New York: Pueblo Publishing Company, 1990, 108–9.

44. *Apostolic Tradition,* 23.7.

45. Ibid., 21.8.

46. Ibid., 26.

47. Ibid., 26.1, 15.

48. Cyprian of Carthage, *On the Lapsed,* 25.

49. Cyprian, Letter 12.1.

50. Echlin, *Deacon,* 38.

51. Cyprian, Letter 5.2. See Hennessey, "Diakonia," 76.

52. Letter 41.1, 4.

53. Letter 52.1.

54. McPartlan, "Catholic and Ecumenical Perspectives," 13.

55. Eusebius, *History of the Church,* 6.43.11.

56. Hennessey, "Diakonia," 84.

57. Chadwick, *Early Church,* 48.

58. Echlin, *Deacon,* 54–55.

59. *Egeria's Travels to the Holy Land,* 24.5–6, rev. ed., tr. John Wilkinson, Warminster, England: Aris and Phillips, 1981, 124.

60. Echlin, *Deacon,* 66

61. Barnett, *The Diaconate,* 79.

62. McPartlan, "Catholic and Ecumenical Perspectives," 13. See also Hennessey, "Diakonia," 85.

63. Introduction to the *Ratio,* and *Directory,* #2.

64. McPartlan, "Catholic and Ecumenical Perspectives," 14; see also *Ratio,* 2.

65. Bishop Ostuni quoted in Echlin, *Deacon,* 100.

66. Ibid.

67. Brockman, *Ordained to Service,* 30.

68. A précis of Schamoni's notes is available in Josef Hornef, "The Genesis and Growth of the Proposal," in *Foundations for the Renewal of the Diaconate,* Washington, D.C.: United States Conference of Catholic Bishops, 1993, 9–11. Schamoni later wrote a book on the topic, published in English as *Married Men as Ordained Deacons,* London: Burns and Oates, 1955.

Chapter 5

1. Santer, "Diaconate and Discipleship," 179.

2. *Ratio,* #9–10.

3. For example, see Michael McHugh, "Lawrence," in *Encyclopedia of Early Christianity,* ed. Everett Ferguson, 2nd ed., vol. 2, New York and London: Garland Publishing Company, 1997, 668.

4. Vincent L. Kennedy, *The Saints of the Canon of the Mass,* 2nd ed., Città del Vaticano: Pontificio Istituto Di Archeologia Cristiana, 1963, 134.

5. William McCarthy, "Prudentius, Peristephanon 2: Vapor and the Martyrdom of Lawrence," *Vigiliae Christianae* 36 (1982): 283.

6. See Sister M. Clement Eagan, C.C.V.I., tr., "Hymn in Honor of the Passion of the Blessed Martyr Lawrence," in *The Poems of Prudentius,* Washington, D.C.: The Catholic University of America Press, 1962, pp. 111–12, lines 141–44, 157–60. There is an interesting study of the entire hymn by Catherine Conybeare in "The Ambiguous Laughter of Saint Laurence," *Journal of Early Christian Studies* 10 (2002): 175–202.

7. Eagan , pp. 116–117, lines 281–84.

8. Sidney H. Griffith, S.T., "Ephraem, The Deacon of Edessa, and the Church of the Empire," in *Diakonia, Studies in Honor of Robert T. Meyer,* ed. Thomas Halton and Joseph Williman, Washington, D.C.: The Catholic University of America Press, 1986, 22–52. Also Griffith, "A Spiritual Father for the Whole Church, St. Ephraem the Syrian," *Sobornost* 20 (1998): 27. Finally, see also Paul S. Russell, "St. Ephraem, The Syrian Theologian," *Pro Ecclesia* 7 (1998): 82.

9. Peter Robson, "Ephrem as a Poet," in *Horizons in Semitic Studies,* ed. John H. Eaton, Birmingham, U.K.: University of Birmingham, Dept. of Theology, 1980, 34–35.

10. For example, see Sebastian Brock, *The Harp of the Spirit: Eighteen Poems of St. Ephrem,* Oxford: The Fellowship of St. Alban and St. Sergius, 1975; also Kathleen McVey, ed., *Ephrem the Syrian: Hymns,* Mahwah, N.J.: Paulist Press, 1989.

11. Brock, "The Oriental Fathers," in *Early Christianity: Origins and Evolution to AD 600,* (Festschrift for W. H. C. Frend), Ian Hazlett, ed., London: S.P.C.K., 1991, 163.

12. Robert Murray, S.J., *Symbols of Church and Kingdom: A Study in Early Syriac Tradition,* Cambridge: Cambridge University Press, 1975, 31.

13. Ephrem, "Hymn on the Nativity, No. 14," in *Nicene and Post-Nicene Fathers,* tr. A. E. Johnston, 2nd series, vol. 13, Grand Rapids, Mich.: Eerdmans, 1964, 251–52.

14. Ephrem, "Hymns on Faith, No. 1," in Brock, *Harp of the Spirit,* 7.

15. Murray, *Symbols,* 89.

16. Ephrem, "Hymns on the Nativity," 13.7, in McVey, *Ephrem the Syrian,* 138.

17. Ibid., 30–31.

18. Ephrem, "Hymns on Virginity," 37.2, in Sebastian P. Brock, *Studies in Syriac Spirituality,* Poona, India: The Syrian Churches Series, 1988, 105–106.

19. Lash, "Ministry of the Word or Comedy and Philology," *New Blackfriars* 68 (1987): 477.

20. Walter Burghardt, *Preaching: The Art and Craft,* Mahwah, N.J.: Paulist Press, 1987, 10.

21. Santer, "Diaconate and Discipleship," 181.

22. Cited in Michael de la Bedoyere, *Francis: A Biography of the Saint of Assisi,* New York and Evanston, Ill.: Harper & Row, 1962, 224.

23. Michael Robson, *St. Francis of Assisi: The Legend and the Life,* London: Geoffrey Chapman, 1997, 227.

24. John Saward, *Perfect Fools,* Oxford: Oxford University Press, 1980, 84.

25. See Gordon Leff, *Heresy in the Middle Ages,* Manchester, U.K.: Manchester University Press, 1999, 51–166.

26. Joseph H. Lynch, *The Medieval Church: A Brief History,* London and New York: Longman, 1992, 231.

27. Saward, *Perfect Fools,* 85.

28. Duane V. Lapsanski, "Francis of Assisi: An Approach to Franciscan Spirituality," in *The Spirituality of Western Christendom,* ed. E. Rozanne Elder, Kalamazoo, Mich.: Cistercian Publications, 1976, 121.

29. Saward, *Perfect Fools,* 1.

30. Louis K. Dupre, *The Deeper Life: An Introduction to Christian Mysticism,* New York: Crossroad, 1981, 55.

31. Anton Rotzetter, O.F.M.Cap., "The Basic Experience," in *Gospel Living: Francis of Assisi Yesterday and Today,* by Anton Rotzetter, O.F.M.Cap., Willibrord-Christian Van Dijk, O.F.M.Cap., and Thadee Matura, O.F.M., New York: St. Bonaventure University–The Franciscan Institute, 1994, 116.

32. Ibid., 125.

33. *Ratio,* #22, quoting the *Directory on the Applications of the Principles and Norms on Ecumenism* (1993), 71.

34. See the brief biography of "Ferrar, Nicholas" by Mandell Creighton in *The Dictionary of National Biography,* vol. VI, Oxford: Oxford University Press, original publication date 1889, reprinted 1921–22, 1241–44.

35. Santer, "Diaconate and Discipleship," 181.

36. Creighton, "Ferrar, Nicholas," 1241.

37. Alan L. Maycock, *Nicholas Ferrar of Little Gidding,* Grand Rapids, Mich:: Eerdmans, 1980, 49. The original date of publication is 1938.

38. "Ferrar, Nicholas," in *The Oxford Dictionary of the Christian Church,* ed. Frank L. Cross and Elizabeth A. Livingstone, 2nd ed., Oxford: Oxford University Press, 1974, 508.

39. Maycock, *Nicholas Ferrar,* 120.

40. Ibid., 130.

41. "Little Gidding," in *The Oxford Dictionary,* ed. Cross and Livingstone, 828.

42. Maycock, *Nicholas Ferrar,* 201.

43. Creighton, "Ferrar, Nicholas," 1242.

44. Maycock, *Nicholas Ferrar,* 156.

45. Ibid., 190.

46. Ibid., 232.

47. Ibid., 234.

48. Ibid.

49. Ibid., 235.

50. Ibid., 239.

51. A. L. Maycock, *Chronicles of Little Gidding,* London: 1954, 3.

52. Cited in A. M. Allchin, *The Joy of All Creation,* Cambridge, Mass.: Cowley Publications, 1984, 57.

53. Maycock, *Nicholas Ferrar,* 4, 144.

Chapter 6

1. Msgr. James Moroney, "Be Imbued with the Spirit and Power of the Liturgy: *Agnosce, Imitare, Conforma.*" This is an unpublished paper for the Bishops' Committee on the Liturgy, 2000. The original text refers to priests only. I have adapted it to refer also to deacons.

2. Fergus Kerr, O.P., "Liturgy and Impersonality," *New Blackfriars* 52 (1971): 436.

3. Msgr. Francis Mannion, "Agendas for Liturgical Reform," *America* 175 (November 30, 1996): 15–16.

4. Abbott, *Documents,* 144.

5. Moroney, "Be Imbued," 4.

6. David W. Fagerberg, "On the Reform of Liturgists," *Antiphon: A Journal for Liturgical Renewal* 5 (2000): 6–7.

7. *Directory,* #29.

8. E. D. Hirsch, *Cultural Literacy,* Boston: Houghton Mifflin, 1987, xv.

9. Paul McPartlan, "The Eucharist, the Church and Evangelization," *Communio* 23 (1996): 782.

10. See Owen F. Cummings, *Eucharistic Soundings,* Dublin: Veritas Publications, 1999, 95–106.

11. See David Tracy, *The Analogical Imagination,* London: SCM Press, 1981, 193–230, 371–90, 405–28.

12. David Martin, *The Breaking of the Image,* New York: St. Martin's Press, 1979, 82.

13. Abbott, *Documents,* 146.

14. Anthony Ruff, O.S.B., "The General Instruction 2000," *Antiphon: A Journal for Liturgical Renewal* 5 (2000): 5.

15. See Msgr. Francis Mannion, "Catholic Worship and the Dynamics of Congregationalism," *Chicago Studies* 33 (1994): 59.

16. *Directory,* #30.

17. Ruff, "General Instruction," 6.

18. Moroney, "Be Imbued," 6.

19. David N. Power, O.M.I., "Vatican II and the Liturgical Future," *Antiphon: A Journal for Liturgical Renewal* 5 (2000): 14.

20. Ruff, "General Instruction," 6.

21. The address is summarized in several columns of *Origins* 31 (2001): 38–40.

22. Ibid., 38–39.

23. Ibid., 39.

24. Of course, a deacon's liturgical rites and obligations go well beyond his assistance at Mass. A comprehensive account may be had in Michael Kwatera, O.S.B., *The Liturgical Ministry of Deacons,* Collegeville, Minn.: The Liturgical Press, 1985. Comprehensive though this is, it was written before the revised G.I.R.M.

25. *Directory,* #54.

Chapter 7

1. Robert Barron, *The Strangest Way: Walking the Christian Path,* Maryknoll, N.Y.: Orbis Books, 2002, 13.

2. Ibid., 32.

3. An essay by the Australian Catholic theologian Denis Edwards has been of immense help in this chapter: "Personal Symbol of Communion," in *The Spirituality of the Diocesan Priest,* ed. Donald B. Cozzens, Collegeville, Minn.: The Liturgical Press, 1997, 73–84.

4. Ibid., 78.

5. Barron, *Strangest Way,* 48.

6. Barron, *Strangest Way,* 53.

7. For the notion of "re-reading," see Louis K. Dupre, *The Other Dimension: An Introduction to Christian Mysticism,* New York: Crossroad, 1981, 25–29.

8. David F. Ford, *The Shape of Living,* London: Harper Collins, 1997, 90.

9. Gerard W. Hughes, S.J., *God of Surprises,* London: Darton, Longman and Todd, 1985, 41.

10. *Ratio,* #74.

11. Michael Casey, O.C.S.O., *Sacred Reading: The Ancient Art of Lectio Divina,* Liguori, Mo.: Liguori–Triumph Books, 1995, 31.

12. *Ratio,* #75.

13. Jaap van Klinken, *Diakonia,* Grand Rapids, Mich.: Eerdmans, 1989, 50.

14. The book *The Spirituality of the Psalms* was edited by Carol Dempsey, O.P., and Timothy Lenchak, S.V.D., Collegeville, Minn.: The Liturgical Press, 2002. The two essays, "The Psalms, Heart of the Liturgy" and "The Psalms, Prayer Within Reality," are from Stuhlmueller's book of biblical theology, *Thirsting for the Lord: Essays in Biblical Spirituality,* New York: Alba House, 1977, 147–62, 163–78.

15. Stuhlmueller, *The Spirituality of the Psalms,* 11. The seven principles come from pages 9–24.

16. Artur Weiser, *The Psalms,* tr. H. Hartwell, Philadelphia: The Westminster Press, 1962.

17. Ibid., 577.

18. John G. Davies, *Pilgrimage Yesterday and Today,* London: SCM Press, 1988, 184–85.

19. Cited in Barron, *Strangest Way,* 72.

20. Ibid.

21. Ibid., 85.

22. Ibid., 100.

23. Alan Jones, *Soul Making,* London: SCM Press, 1985, 41.

Chapter 8

1. Richard Gaillardetz, "Learning from Marriage," *Commonweal* 127 (September 8, 2000): 21.

2. Abbott, *Documents,* 56.

3. Ibid., 250–253.

4. *Catechism of the Catholic Church,* Liguori, Mo.: Liguori Publications, 1994, §1601–66.

5. Quoted by Thomas K. Carroll, *Wisdom and Wasteland: Jeremy Taylor in His Prose and Preaching Today*, Dublin: Four Courts Press, 2001, 133–45.

6. Edmund Newey, "Jeremy Taylor and the Theology of Marriage," *Anglican Theological Review* 84 (2001): 273.

7. Carroll, *Wisdom and Wasteland*, 133.

8. Newey, "Jeremy Taylor," 271.

9. Paragraph 48, in Abbott, *Documents*, 250.

10. Carroll, *Wisdom and Wasteland*, 135.

11. Ibid.

12. Ibid.

13. Newey, "Jeremy Taylor, 275.

14. Par. 48, in Abbott, *Documents*, 250.

15. Carroll, *Wisdom and Wasteland*, 138.

16. Ibid., 139.

17. Ibid., 140.

18. Ibid., 142–43.

19. Quotations from the rites of marriage and ordination are drawn from *The Rites of the Catholic Church*, 2 vols., New York: Pueblo Publishing Company, 1976, 1980.

20. Paul VI, *Humanae Vitae*, par. 9, 1968.

21. *Ratio*, #68.

22. Ibid., #5.

23. Karl Rahner, "The Theology of the Restoration of the Diaconate," in *Foundations for the Renewal of the Diaconate*, Washington, D.C.: United States Conference of Catholic Bishops, 1993, 163.

24. For a fine theological reading of the novel, see Robert McAfee Brown, *Persuade Us to Rejoice: The Liberating Power of Fiction*, Louisville, Ky.: Westminster John Knox Press, 1992, 102–11.

25. Alan Paton, *Too Late the Phalarope*, New York: Charles Scribner's Sons, 1953, 88.

26. Robert McAfee Brown, *Spirituality and Liberation*, London: Hodder and Stoughton, 1988, 99–100.

27. Ibid., 102.

28. I owe these most helpful references on the work of Paton, Kierkegaard, and Buber to the very insightful *Spirituality and Liberation* of Robert McAfee Brown, especially chapter 7.

29. Martin Buber, *Between Man and Man,* New York: Macmillan, 1965, 52.

30. George Herbert, *The Complete English Poems,* ed. John Tobin, Harmondsworth, U.K.: Penguin Books, 1991, 169.

31. Barron, *Strangest Way,* 97.

32. Archbishop Rowan Williams of Canterbury, "The Body's Grace," in *Our Selves, Our Souls and Bodies,* ed. Charles Hefling, Boston: Cowley Publications, 1996, 59.

Chapter 9

1. Ormonde Plater, *Many Servants: An Introduction to Deacons,* Cambridge, Mass.: Cowley Publications, 1991, 204.

2. Bishop John F. Kinney, "Diaconal Service in Pastoral Ministry," Proceedings of the National Catholic Diaconate Conference, July 20–23, 1994, *Deacon Digest* 11 (1994), 17.

3. Aidan Kavanagh, O.S.B., *Elements of Rite: A Handbook of Liturgical Style,* New York: Pueblo Publishing Co., 1982, 75.

4. Ibid., 76.

5. Bishop Dale Melczek, "Keynote Conference Address on the Permanent Diaconate," Proceedings of the National Catholic Diaconate Conference, July 20–23, 1994, *Deacon Digest* 11 (1994), 12.

6. Quoted by William Shawn McKnight in *The Latin Rite Deacon: Symbol of Communitas and Social Intermediary Among the People of God,* Rome: Pontificium Athenaeum S. Anselmi, 2001, 45.

7. *Ratio,* #84.

8. Frances M. Young, *Can These Dry Bones Live? The Excitement of Theological Study,* London: SCM Press, 1992, 2.

9. Aidan Nichols, *The Shape of Catholic Theology,* Collegeville, Minn.: The Liturgical Press, 1991, 19.

10. Frances M. Young, in the Foreword to *Focus on God,* London: Epworth Press, 1986.

11. Joanna Trollope, *The Rector's Wife,* New York: Random House, 1993. See the excellent review by Victoria J. Barnett in *Christian Century* 112 (January 18, 1995): 60–63.

12. Ibid., 62.

Chapter 10

1. Adapted to include deacons from Andrew M. Greeley, "A Catholic Revival?" *America* 180 (April 10, 1999): 8, 14.

2. Yves Congar, *This Church That I Love,* Denville, N.J.: Dimension Books, 1969, especially 83–100.

3. John C. Cavadini, "Levels of Trust," *Notre Dame Magazine* (Summer 2002): 23.

4. Gerard M. Hopkins, S.J., "God's Grandeur," in *Gerard Manley Hopkins: Poems and Prose,* ed. W. H. Gardner, Harmondsworth, U.K.: Penguin Books, 1985, 27.

5. Augustine, *The City of God,* 14.3.

6. John Macquarrie, *Theology, Church and Ministry,* London: SCM Press, 1986, 109.

7. Ibid., 112.

8. Congar, *This Church,* 87.

9. Cummings, *Eucharistic Soundings,* 121–29.

10. Abbott, *Documents,* 55.

11. Pope John Paul II, *Centesimus Annus,* par. 5.

12. Abbott, *Documents,* 56.

13. Jean Daniélou, S.J., *Why the Church?* Chicago: Franciscan Herald Press, 1975, 141.

Bibliography

Abbott, Walter M., S.J., ed. *The Documents of Vatican II.* New York: Herder and Herder, 1966.

Audet, Jean Paul. *Structures in Christian Priesthood.* New York: Macmillan, 1967.

Barnett, James M. *The Diaconate, A Full and Equal Order.* Rev. ed. Valley Forge, Pa.: Trinity Press International, 1995.

Barnett, Victoria. "Review of Joanna Trollope, *The Rector's Wife.*" In *Christian Century* 112 (January 18, 1995): 60–63.

Barron, Robert. *The Strangest Way: Walking the Christian Path.* Maryknoll, N.Y.: Orbis Books, 2002.

Bedoyere, Michael de la. *Francis: A Biography of the Saint of Assisi.* New York and Evanston, Ill.: Harper & Row, 1962.

Bradshaw, Paul F. *Liturgical Presidency in the Early Church.* Bramcote, Notts., U.K.: Grove Books, 1983.

———. *Ordination Rites of the Ancient Churches of East and West.* New York: Pueblo Publishing Company, 1990.

Brock, Sebastian P. *The Harp of the Spirit: Eighteen Poems of St. Ephrem.* Oxford: The Fellowship of St. Alban and St. Sergius, 1975.

———. *Studies in Syriac Spirituality.* Poona, India: The Syrian Churches Series, 1988.

———. "The Oriental Fathers." In *Early Christianity: Origins and Evolution to AD 600* (Festschrift for W. H. C. Frend), edited by Ian Hazlett, 163–72. Nashville: Abingdon Press, 1991.

Brockman, Norbert, S.M. *Ordained to Service: A Theology of the Permanent Diaconate.* Smithtown, N.Y.: Exposition Press, 1976.

Brown, Raymond E., S.S. *Priest and Bishop: Biblical Reflections.* London: Geoffrey Chapman, 1971.

Brown, Robert McAfee. *Spirituality and Liberation.* London: Hodder and Stoughton, 1988.

————. *Persuade Us to Rejoice: The Liberating Power of Fiction.* Louisville, Ky.: Westminster John Knox Press, 1992.

Buber, Martin. *Between Man and Man.* New York: Macmillan, 1965.

Burghardt, Walter J., S.J. *Preaching: The Art and Craft.* New York/Mahwah, N.J.: Paulist Press, 1987.

Carroll, Colleen. *The New Faithful.* Chicago: Loyola Press, 2002.

Carroll, Thomas K. *Wisdom and Wasteland: Jeremy Taylor in His Prose and Preaching Today.* Dublin: Four Courts Press, 2001.

Casey, Michael, O.C.S.O. *Sacred Reading: The Ancient Art of Lectio Divina.* Liguori, Mo.: Liguori–Triumph Books, 1995.

Cavadini, John C. "Levels of Trust." *Notre Dame Magazine* (Summer 2002): 20–25.

Catechism of the Catholic Church. Liguori, Mo.: Liguori Publications, 1994.

Chadwick, Henry. *The Early Church.* Rev. ed. Harmondsworth, U.K.: Penguin Books, 1993.

Collins, John N. *Diakonia, Reinterpreting the Ancient Sources.* New York: Oxford University Press, 1990.

————. *Are All Christians Ministers?* Newtown, New South Wales: E. J. Dwyer, 1992.

————. "Learning About Ministry from the Seven." *Deacon Digest* (May/June, 1998): 26–30.

Congar, Yves, O.P. *This Church That I Love.* Denville, N.J.: Dimension Books, 1969.

Congregation for Catholic Education. *Basic Norms for the Formation of Permanent Deacons.* Vatican City: Libreria Editrice Vaticana, 1998.

Congregation for the Clergy. *Directory for the Ministry and Life of Permanent Deacons.* Vatican City: Libreria Editrice Vaticana, 1998.

Conybeare, Catherine. "The Ambiguous Laughter of St. Laurence." *Journal of Early Christian Studies* 10 (2002): 175–202.

Creighton, Mandell. "Ferrar, Nicholas." In *The Dictionary of National Biography,* vol. VI, 1241–1244. Oxford: Oxford University Press, 1921–22.

Croce, Walter, S.J. "From the History of the Diaconate." In *Foundations for the Renewal of the Permanent Diaconate,* 61–89. Washington, D.C.: United States Conference of Catholic Bishops, 1993.

Cross, Frank Leslie. *The Early Christian Fathers.* London: Duckworth, 1960.

Cummings, Owen F. "Friedrich von Hügel and Today's Seminarian." *Seminary Journal* 3 (1997): 57–60.

———. *Eucharistic Soundings.* Dublin: Veritas Publications, 1999.

———. *John Macquarrie, A Master of Theology.* New York/Mahwah, N.J.: Paulist Press, 2002.

Danielou, Jean, S.J. *Why the Church?* Chicago: Franciscan Herald Press, 1975.

Davies, John G. "Deacons, Deaconesses and the Minor Orders in the Patristic Church." *Journal of Ecclesiastical History* 13 (1962): 1–15.

Donovan, William T. *The Sacrament of Service: Understanding Diaconal Spirituality.* Green Bay, Wis.: Alt Publishing Co., 2000.

Doyle, Dennis M. *The Church as Communion.* Maryknoll, N.Y.: Orbis Books, 2000.

Dulles, Avery R., S.J. *The Reshaping of Catholicism.* San Francisco: Harper & Row, 1988.

———. "The Four Faces of American Catholicism." *Louvain Studies* 18 (1993): 99–109.

Dupre, Louis K. *The Deeper Life: An Introduction to Christian Mysticism.* New York: Crossroad, 1981.

Eagan, Sister M. Clement, C.C.V.I., trans. "Hymn in Honor of the Passion of the Blessed Martyr Lawrence." In *The Poems of Prudentius,* 111–12. Washington, D.C.: The Catholic University of America Press, 1962.

Echlin, Edward P., S.J. *The Deacon in the Church, Past and Future.* New York: Alba House, 1971.

Edwards, Denis. "Personal Symbol of Communion." In *The Spirituality of the Diocesan Priest,* edited by Donald B. Cozzens, 73–84. Collegeville, Minn.: The Liturgical Press, 1997.

Emilsen, William W. "The Face of Christ: The Ministry of Deacons." *The Expository Times* 110 (April 1999): 216–17.

Fagerberg, David W. "On the Reform of Liturgists." *Antiphon: A Journal for Liturgical Renewal* 5 (2000): 5–7.

Ferguson, Everett, ed. *Encyclopedia of Early Christianity.* New York and London: Garland Publishing Company, 1990.

Ford, David F. *The Shape of Living.* London: Harper Collins, 1997.

Gaillardetz, Richard. "Learning from Marriage." *Commonweal* 127 (September 8, 2000): 18–21.

George, Francis, O.M.I. "The Bishop and His Deacons." *Deacon Digest* 16 (May/June 1999): 9–11.

Greeley, Andrew M. "A Catholic Revival?" *America* 180 (April 10, 1999): 8–14.

Griffith, Sidney H., S.T. "Ephraem, the Deacon of Edessa, and the Church of the Empire." In *Diakonia, Studies in Honor of Robert T. Meyer,* edited by Thomas P. Halton and Joseph P. Williman, 22–52. Washington, D.C.: The Catholic University of America Press, 1986.

———. "A Spiritual Father for the Whole Church, St. Ephraem the Syrian." *Sobornost* 20 (1998): 21–40.

Harrington, Daniel J., S.J. *The Church According to the New Testament.* Franklin, Wis.: Sheed and Ward, 2001.

Heaney, John J. *The Modernist Crisis: Von Hügel.* Washington, D.C.: Corpus Books, 1968.

Hennessey, Lawrence R., S.T. "Diakonia and Diakonos in the Pre-Nicene Church." In *Diakonia: Studies in Honor of Robert T. Meyer,* edited by Thomas Halton and Joseph P. Williman, 60–86. Washington, D.C.: The Catholic University of America Press, 1986.

Herbert, George. *The Complete English Poems,* edited by John Tobin. Harmondsworth, U.K.: Penguin Books, 1991.

Hopkins, Gerard Manley. *Gerard Manley Hopkins: Poems and Prose.* Ed. W. H. Gardner. Harmondsworth, U.K.: Penguin Books, 1985.

Hornef, Josef. "The Genesis and Growth of the Proposal." In *Foundations for the Renewal of the Diaconate*, 5–27. Washington, D.C.: United States Conference of Catholic Bishops, 1993.

Howatch, Susan. *Absolute Truths*. New York: Fawcett, 1995.

Hughes, Gerard W., S.J. *God of Surprises*. London: Darton, Longman and Todd, 1985.

Jewett, Robert. "Paul, Phoebe and the Spanish Mission." In *The Social World of Formative Christianity and Judaism*, edited by Jacob Neusner and others, 142–61. Philadelphia: Fortress Press, 1988.

John Paul II. *On the Coming of the Third Millennium*. Washington, D.C.: United States Conference of Catholic Bishops, 1994.

———. *Novo Millennio Ineunte*. Washington, D.C.: United States Conference of Catholic Bishops, 2001.

Kasper, Walter. "The Deacon Offers an Ecclesiological View of the Present Day Challenges in the Church and Society." Paper presented at the International Diaconate Center Study-Conference, Brixen, Italy, October 1997. Available at www.deacons.net.

Kavanagh, Aidan, O.S.B. *Elements of Rite: A Handbook of Liturgical Style*. New York: Pueblo Publishing Co., 1982.

Kennedy, Vincent L. *The Saints of the Canon of the Mass*. 2nd ed. Citta del Vaticano: Pontificio Istituto di Archeologia Cristiana, 1963.

Kerkwoorde, Augustinus, O.S.B. "The Theology of the Diaconate." In *Foundations for the Renewal of the Permanent Diaconate*, 90–138. Washington, D.C.: United States Conference of Catholic Bishops, 1993.

Kerr, Fergus, O.P. "Liturgy and Impersonality." *New Blackfriars* 52 (1971): 436–47.

Kinney, John F. "Diaconal Service in Pastoral Ministry." Proceedings of the National Catholic Diaconal Conference, July 20–23, 1994. *Deacon Digest* 11 (1994): 15–18.

Kramer, Hannes. "The Spiritual Life of the Deacon." In *Foundations for the Renewal of the Permanent Diaconate*, 28–50. Washington, D.C.: United States Conference of Catholic Bishops, 1993.

Kwatera, Michael, O.S.B. *The Liturgical Ministry of Deacons.* Collegeville, Minn.: The Liturgical Press, 1985.

Lapsanski, Duane V. "Francis of Assisi: An Approach to Franciscan Spirituality." In *The Spirituality of Western Christendom,* edited by E. Rozanne Elder, 116–24. Kalamazoo, Mich.: Cistercian Publications, 1976.

Lash, Nicholas. "Ministry of the Word or Comedy and Philology." *New Blackfriars* 68 (1987): 472–83.

———. "The Difficulty of Making Sense." *New Blackfriars* 70 (1989): 74–84.

Leff, Gordon. *Heresy in the Middle Ages.* Manchester: Manchester University Press, 1999.

Lynch, Joseph H. *The Medieval Church: A Brief History.* London and New York: Longman, 1992.

Macquarrie, John. *Theology, Church and Ministry.* London: SCM Press, 1986.

Mannion, Msgr. Francis. "Catholic Worship and the Dynamics of Congregationalism." *Chicago Studies* 33 (1994): 57–66.

———. "Agendas for Liturgical Reform." *America* 175 (November 30, 1996): 9–16.

Martimort, Aimé-George. *Deaconesses: An Historical Study.* San Francisco: Ignatius Press, 1986.

Matera, Frank J. *New Testament Christology.* Louisville, Ky.: Westminster John Knox Press, 1999.

Maycock, Alan L. *Nicholas Ferrar of Little Gidding.* Grand Rapids, Mich.: Eerdmans, 1980.

McCarthy, William. "Prudentius, Peristephanon 2: Vapor and the Martyrdom of Lawrence." *Vigiliae Christianae* 36 (1982): 382–86.

McHugh, Michael P. "Lawrence." In *Encyclopedia of Early Christianity,* edited by Everett Ferguson, vol. 2, p. 668. 2nd ed. New York and London: Garland Publishing Co., 1997.

McKnight, William Shawn. *The Latin Rite Deacon: Symbol of Communitas and Social Intermediary Among the People of God.* Rome: Pontificium Athenaeum S. Anselmi, 2001.

McNamara, Kevin, ed. *The Church: A Theological and Pastoral Commentary on the Constitution on the Church.* Dublin: Veritas Publications, 1983.

McPartlan, Paul. "Diaconate." In *The Oxford Companion to Christian Thought,* edited by Adrian Hastings and others, 166–67. Oxford: Oxford University Press, 2000.

———. "The Permanent Diaconate and *Gaudium et Spes.*" *Briefing* 32 (2002): 3–10.

———. "The Permanent Diaconate: Catholic and Ecumenical Perspectives." *Briefing* 32 (2002): 10–16.

McVey, Kathleen, ed. *Ephrem the Syrian: Hymns.* New York/ Mahwah, N.J.: Paulist Press, 1989.

Melczek, Dale. "Keynote Conference Address on the Permanent Diaconate." Proceedings of the National Catholic Diaconate Conference, July 20–23, 1994. *Deacon Digest* 11 (1994): 11–14.

Moroney, James. "Be Imbued with the Spirit and Power of the Liturgy: *Agnosce, Imitare, Conforma.*" Unpublished paper for the Bishops' Committee on the Liturgy, 2000.

———. "The Deacon and the Liturgy." *Origins* 31 (2001): 38–40.

Murray, Robert, S.J. *Symbols of Church and Kingdom.* Cambridge: Cambridge University Press, 1975.

Newey, Edmund. "Jeremy Taylor and the Theology of Marriage." *Anglican Theological Review* 84 (2001): 269–85.

Nichols, Aidan, O.P. *The Shape of Catholic Theology.* Collegeville, Minn.: The Liturgical Press, 1991.

Osborne, Kenan B., O.F.M. *The Diaconate in the Christian Church: Its History and Theology.* Chicago: National Association of Diaconate Directors, 1996.

Paton, Alan. *Too Late the Phalarope.* New York: Charles Scribner's Sons, 1953.

Plater, Ormonde. *Many Servants: An Introduction to Deacons.* Cambridge, Mass.: Cowley Publications, 1991.

Power, David N., O.M.I. "Vatican II and the Liturgical Future." *Antiphon: A Journal for Liturgical Renewal* 5 (2000): 10–18.

Rahner, Karl, S.J. "The Teaching of the Second Vatican Council on the Diaconate." In *Foundations for the Renewal of the Permanent Diaconate,* 182–92. Washington, D.C.: United States Conference of Catholic Bishops, 1993.

———. "The Theology of the Restoration of the Diaconate." In *Foundations for the Renewal of the Permanent Diaconate*, 139–81. Washington, D.C.: United States Conference of Catholic Bishops, 1993.

———. "On the Diaconate." In *Foundations for the Renewal of the Permanent Diaconate*, 193–212. Washington, D.C.: United States Conference of Catholic Bishops, 1993.

Reardon, Bernard M. G. *Roman Catholic Modernism*. Stanford, Calif.: Stanford University Press, 1970.

Robson, Michael, O.F.M.Conv. *St. Francis of Assisi: The Legend and the Life*. London: Geoffrey Chapman, 1997.

Robson, Peter. "Ephrem as a Poet." In *Horizons in Semitic Studies*, edited by John H. Eaton, 15–22. Birmingham, U.K.: University of Birmingham, Dept. of Theology, 1980.

Rotzetter, Anton, O.F.M.Cap., Willibrord-Christian van Dijk, O.F.M.Cap., and Thadee Matura, O.F.M. *Gospel Living: Francis of Assisi, Yesterday and Today*. New York: St. Bonaventure University–The Franciscan Institute, 1994.

Ruff, Anthony, O.S.B. "The General Instruction 2000." *Antiphon: A Journal for Liturgical Renewal* 5 (2000): 5–7.

Russell, Paul S. "St. Ephraem, The Syrian Theologian." *Pro Ecclesia* 7 (1998): 79–90.

Santer, Mark. "Diaconate and Discipleship." *Theology* 81 (1978): 179–82.

Saward, John. *Perfect Fools*. Oxford: Oxford University Press, 1980.

Senn, Frank C. "The Ecclesiological Basis of the Office of Deacon." *Pro Ecclesia* 3 (1994): 197–205.

Suenens, Leon J. *Co-responsibility in the Church*. New York: Herder and Herder, 1968.

Tracy, David. *The Analogical Imagination*. New York: Crossroad, 1981.

———. "Freedom, Responsibility, Authority." In *Empowering Authority: The Charisms of Episcopacy and Primacy in the Church Today*, edited by Patrick J. Howell and Gary Chamberlain, 32–45. Kansas City, Mo.: Sheed and Ward, 1990.

Trevor, Meriol. *Prophets and Guardians: Renewal and Tradition in the Church*. Garden City, N.Y.: Doubleday, 1969.

Trollope, Joanna. *The Rector's Wife*. New York: Random House, 1993.

van Klinken, Jaap. *Diakonia*. Grand Rapids, Mich.: Eerdmans, 1989.

Vanstone, William. *Love's Endeavour, Love's Expense*. London: Darton, Longman and Todd, 1977.

von Hugel, Friedrich. *The Mystical Element of Religion*, 2 vols. London: Dent, 1908.

————. *Eternal Life*. Edinburgh: T. & T. Clark, 1912.

————. *Essays and Addresses*, 2 vols. London: Dent, 1921.

————. *Selected Letters*, edited by B. Holland. London: Dent, 1927.

Williams, Rowan D. "The Body's Grace." In *Our Selves, Our Souls and Bodies*, edited by Charles Hefling, 58–68. Boston: Cowley Publications, 1996.

Witherington, Ben, III. *The Many Faces of Christ*. New York: Crossroad, 1998.

Wood, Susan K. *Sacramental Orders*. Collegeville, Minn.: The Liturgical Press, 2000.

Young, Frances M. *Focus on God*. London: Epworth Press, 1986.

————. *Can These Dry Bones Live? The Excitement of Theological Study*. London: SCM Press, 1992.